True Success

OTHER BOOKS BY ARNOLD S. JUDSON

A Manager's Guide to Making Changes
John Wiley & Sons, London, 1966

Changing Behavior in Organizations
Blackwell, Oxford 1991

Making Strategy Happen
Blackwell, Oxford 1996

True Success

What It Means and How Organizations Can Achieve It

Arnold S. Judson
Author of Making Strategy Happen and Changing
Behavior in Organizations

iUniverse, Inc.
New York Lincoln Shanghai

True Success
What It Means and How Organizations Can Achieve It

Copyright © 2007 by Arnold S. Judson

iUniverse books may be ordered through booksellers or by contacting:

iUniverse
2021 Pine Lake Road, Suite 100
Lincoln, NE 68512
www.iuniverse.com
1-800-Authors (1-800-288-4677)

The information, ideas, and suggestions in this book are not intended to render professional advice. Before following any suggestions contained in this book, you should consult your personal accountant or other financial advisor. Neither the author nor the publisher shall be liable or responsible for any loss or damage allegedly arising as a consequence of your use or application of any information or suggestions in this book.

ISBN-13: 978-0-595-40526-8 (pbk)
ISBN-13: 978-0-595-84891-1 (ebk)
ISBN-10: 0-595-40526-6 (pbk)
ISBN-10: 0-595-84891-5 (ebk)

Printed in the United States of America

CONTENTS

LIST OF ILLUSTRATIONS

INTRODUCTION

If you are a senior executive or manager in a formal organization, and want greater leverage for improving your organization's performance, this book is for you. This book is relevant whether you are leading a commercial business, not-for-profit or government organization. If you have not yet achieved but aspire to such positions, you will also find this book useful.

For decades, books about management and business have proliferated. They have tended to focus either on personal self-improvement, or on a particular novel technique, approach or process aimed at enhancing business success. In self-improvement books, individual characteristics required for personal success are described along with how these can be developed and attained. In books where the use of novel techniques are advocated, these are described along with how and why their adoption will lead to better business results.

Yet, it is better performance of the *organization* involved that determines whether or not the individual or new approach can be deemed successful. What does it mean and take for an *organization* to be successful? This is a different, separate issue. Few books have addressed this question.

Although many best selling business books contain good ideas and sound advice, their collective impact on improving *organizational* performance has been hard to detect. The reason, I believe, is that even the best of these books are too simplistic for the complexity of the problem. Their authors tend to ignore, miss or underestimate three fundamental truths about success and organizations:

1. "Success" cannot be defined simply in absolutes (i.e. growth, profits, longevity, etc.). Rather, it is multidimensional and a relative and dynamic concept (today's success can mean failure tomorrow). Furthermore, organizational objectives tend to stem from a combination of the leadership's vision, what may be possible both externally and internally, and the personal goals, interests and constraints of key executives.

2. Any organization with more than a dozen members is highly resistant to change. The larger the organization, the more resistant it is. This is because existing systems, policies, procedures and processes, and especially culture, all combine into a force for maintaining the status quo.

3. Any organization's ability to be successful in achieving its long-term objectives depends on three interrelated but separate capabilities. To attain true success, an organization must:

    a. be able continuously to gain accurate understanding of its external environment and internal dynamics and capabilities, and identify and assess alternative opportunities;

    b. be able to generate creative ideas about how to address opportunities on three levels: long-term vision; specific market offerings; and operating approaches and methods; and

    c. have a navigation and guidance mechanism that enables it to achieve (a) while continuously addressing and capitalizing on opportunities within a rapidly changing external environment. The organization must be able to make durable changes both to its complex macro systems, and to the people within these systems.

All this adds up to an overriding issue. For organizations to achieve success is a problem far more subtle and complex than most business and management book authors are willing to acknowledge. Their "solutions" tend to focus on only one or a few elements of this complexity ... an insufficient number and "mass" to gain the required leverage for change and improvement. Yet despite the impotence of these nostrums, they sell because they play into two special characteristics of American management culture. One is an undying belief that no problem is incapable of some "quick-fix" solution. The other is the tendency to value form over substance. The appearance of doing something (never mind what) is all that matters.

For an organization to achieve true success, I believe that it must have *all four* of the following capabilities:

1. Continuous gathering and interpretation of information, both external and internal, to achieve the understanding needed to identify, assess and address opportunities;

2. An executive mindset that acknowledges and accepts the complexity of the problem, that values continuous learning, that views quick-fixes as suspect, that regards no "solution" as final and durable, and that comprehends that the underlying issue to achieving success is how to change the behavior of both systems and the people who inhabit them;

3. A process for organizational navigation and guidance ... to achieve and maintain focus and momentum for performance improvement; and

4. Personal and organizational skills in analysis, learning and creativity.

All four capabilities are discussed in this book with special emphasis on 3, a system for organizational navigation and guidance (SONG). I believe this subject is the least developed in management literature. A number of good books already treat much of the other three capabilities. However, there is need for an integrative, overarching framework to establish a context for understanding and dealing with how these four capabilities interrelate. Once this is understood, SONG can provide the structure and discipline for integrating and orchestrating the other three capabilities, driving the organization towards achieving true success.

In Chapters 1–4 of the book I lay out the problem of achieving organizational success in all its complexity, and suggest what is required to address it effectively. In the remaining chapters I describe a system and process for navigation and guidance (SONG), and how it works. I also tie in the relationships to capabilities 1,2 & 4 above with references to suggested readings. In Chapters 8 and 9, I deal with the special problems of multi-business organizations and how the system for navigation and guidance must be augmented to deal with these issues.

This book is intended as a guide for leaders and senior managers of any kind of organization who want to improve how their organization performs. Ideas are illustrated by many real-life examples from the business, not-for-profit and government sectors. These stem from my more than 55 years of experience as a supervisor, manager and executive in manufacturing and service organizations, management consultant, and Board member for nonprofit organizations. In my more than four decades of management consulting, I worked with clients in the for- and not-for profit sectors, as well as in government ... in North and Central America, Europe and the Middle East. Since 1968, my consulting has focused on strategic planning and strategic management in both single and multi-business organizations. I have continuously been concerned about how organizations of all sizes can achieve durable changes in their performance. In this book, my intent is to share what I have learned.

Arnold S. Judson
Canton, Massachusetts

CHAPTER 1

LOTS OF SOLUTIONS BUT WHAT'S THE PROBLEM?

The quest for the Holy Grail did not end in the middle ages. The quest continues today, but not by knights wearing armor and riding horses. Today's knights wear three-piece suits and carry advanced degrees. The grail they pursue is the key to "success"—success for organizations, and success for the people who run them.

Every year at least one new book appears, announcing *the key* to success. One year, the key is Total Quality Management. The next year's key is Re-engineering. Other years' keys are Management-By-Walking-Around, or The Learning Organization, or The Flat Organization. These ideas are enthusiastically taken up, only to be dropped and replaced by the following year's offering. Yet despite these books' widespread appeal, it's hard to detect any lasting impact on how organizations actually perform.

What's going on here? Is there something wrong with the way "success" is viewed? Are executives and managers so naive and needy that they are willing to try anything? Are the keys offered to unlock success faulty? Or do the locks keep getting changed so that new keys are continuously needed?

The answer, regrettably, is yes to all of the above. Book authors and publishers are benefiting more than their ever-hopeful readers, managers and executives.

A union steward I once knew in New York's largest electric company had a voice like gravel and a wonderful way of mangling English. Once he voiced an objection during some tough negotiations after managers rattled on at some length to justify their position. He growled, "Wait a minute, I think I'm being *misconscrewed!*"

I believe that the meaning of success and how it can be achieved by organizations are being "misconscrewed" both by those offering ready, single-key "solutions" and by those ready and eager to swallow them.

Defining Success Is Not Simple

Any single-key "solution" presumes that success for an organization can be defined consistently in one-dimensional terms. Success for any organization, for- or not-for-profit, public or private, cannot be defined that simply. Defining success is a slippery and complex matter.

Success Is A Perception

Success is not an objective fact. Rather, it is a perception. The perception can be management's, or employees' and their unions', or it can be that of a variety of outside viewers such as investment analysts, business (or other) publications, potential investors or the general public. The same set of facts can lead to widely varying perceptions. How many times have managements, bullish about their firms' performance, been dismayed by analysts' assessments and the verdict of the stock market? How many times have government officials and bureaucrats, convinced that their agencies and departments were on the right track, been startled by very different conclusions appearing in the media and voiced by politicians? And how many times have entirely different conclusions been reached from the same set of facts by management on the one hand, and its employees (and unions) on the other?

Perceptions about an organization's success stem from a number of unrelated considerations. Some are highly subjective, arising from personal agendas. What accomplishments, for example, are especially important to an organization's leaders? The answer varies widely from one organization to another. Some business leaders focus on revenue growth, and industry dominance. Others are more concerned with the quality of their organizations' market offerings and reputation. Some want to maximize shareholder value or profitability. Outside the business sector, some organizational leaders focus on improving the quality of services. Others are more concerned with lowering costs or expanding programs.

Objective Indicators

Objective measures of success are specific performance indicators. For any organization, no single indicator is sufficient to signal success. It takes a number of such indicators to do the job. Business firms look at revenues, profits, returns on sales, assets and equity, earnings per share, and market or shareholder value along with changes over time in all these indicators.

Objective performance indicators are very different for government and not-for-profit organizations. These look to funding from various sources, number of clients served, operating costs, and budget variances.

Changes In What Defines Success

All considerations for defining an organization's success, objective and subjective, change over time. Leaders change. Their agendas change. External circumstances change: competition; consumer tastes, wants and needs; government regulation; and technology. Internal circumstances also change: skills and know-how; product and service quality; location of facilities; and what employees (and their unions) want and need.

Clearly, defining success is no simple matter. It is complicated and messy. Yet those offering keys to success often ignore this. When success is viewed narrowly and as unchanging, translating into profits, or growth, or returns on investment, any key claimed to ensure success is bound to be simplistic. When that key is meant to apply not only to businesses but also to not-for-profit and government organizations, it begins to look like snake oil.

Keys Don't Fit The Lock

Another side to this problem adds more complications. A truly effective key has to change the way organizations work. And any such change must be lasting.

Basic Organizational Characteristics

In any field where more than a single person is needed to accomplish anything, it is an *organization* that does the achieving. Organizations are more than just formal structures. Every organization is a working *system*. This includes people, departments or functions, policies and procedures, and work processes. These are all the activities needed to perform such tasks as dealing with a customer's order, or paying a bill, or developing a new product or service and bringing it to the marketplace. Organizations also include such formal systems as information, budgets, control and compensation. Particularly important is how *all these pieces relate to one another* from day-to-day as the organization does its work.

Assessing An Organization's Performance

In judging how any organization works, two critical questions must be answered. Is the organization working on the "right" things? "Right" is defined by the organization's goals, objectives and priorities. These concern its intended customers, offerings and desired outcomes. Does the focus of what people, departments, processes and systems are *actually doing* day-to-day, reflect the organization's goals and objectives?

The other critical question is how smoothly and effectively the organization works as it performs its various tasks and delivers its products and services to its customers. Every organization, for-profit, not-for-profit, or government, has actual and potential customers and something (a product or service) it offers to these customers. Business organizations find it relatively easy to define customers and offerings. For other kinds of organizations, these definitions take more work.

A special characteristic of government and not-for-profit organizations makes them very different from business organizations. This is multiple constituencies, some of whom are also customers. Each of these has wants, needs and agendas different from those of the others.

> A social agency I worked with provides rehabilitation through work and employment to emotionally disabled clients. This agency has four different constituencies or customers it must satisfy: clients who are being rehabilitated; their employers and contractors; state and federal funding agencies; and private foundations and other sources which provide added funding. It is a formidable task to sort out what it takes to satisfy these different constituencies, and then make sure that the agency actually delivers what is needed.

Organizations and Change

Any proposed key to success requires changing how organizations work. For most organizations, the notion of "success" implies improved achievements or performance. Most organizations want to improve their performance as they pursue their objectives. Actions taken to improve performance must inevitably change how an organization now works. For desired results, such changes have to be lasting.

But it is extremely difficult to achieve lasting changes in the way any organization works. Organizations, even more than the people who inhabit them, tend to resist changes that threaten the *status quo*. In Chapter 5 I discuss in greater detail the issue of changing organizational systems. This difficulty further brings into question the value of single-key "solutions" to organizational success.

Why Such A Market For Mismatched Keys?

Because defining success is complicated, and changing how organizations work is difficult, any proposed "key" underestimates the problem it is supposed to solve. Yet simplistic nostrums continue to stock managements' bookshelves. Why is this so?

The answer lies deep in the psyches of those who become managers and leaders of organizations, especially American ones. U.S. management is the focus here because it is an extreme example of a particular mind-set and because the U.S. has by far been the largest market for books on management. From my work in Britain and Europe, I found managements, while not entirely immune to this mind-set, more thoughtful and cautious in embracing the latest nostrum.

What is it about the mind-set of American managers that attracts them to ideas that promise *the key* to organizational success? The primary influence in shaping this mind-set is their attitudes toward problems, problem-solving and action.

A Self-Defeating Mind-Set

Success in solving problems is a major determinant for advancement up management ranks. Anyone who has already "made it" or who is well along the way believes that every problem can be solved. The best solutions are simple ones that cut quickly to the heart of the matter. Especially attractive are solutions using a specific tool, method, system or process (typically described with an acronym of no more than three letters). Such "solutions" appeal because they promise to do the job fast, yet call for only minimal effort by the executive deciding to use them. This is the "Look, Ma, no hands!" syndrome. Even for a complex problem, somewhere there is a simple, fast solution … it just takes more ingenuity to find it.

The best way to solve any problem is to take action (preferably by applying the right tool, method, system, etc.). This action should appear as personal, not group, and have such an obvious impact that everyone will not only see the result, but also know who should get credit.

Management Faddism

For the past half-century in the U.S. this mind-set has produced a history of faddism. New ideas, seen as panaceas, have been taken up widely with enthusiasm and great expectations, only to be dropped after a year or two and replaced by the next "key".

In my career, first in management and later in consulting, I experienced more than two dozen such fads. When I first went to work in 1948, it was JIT (job instructor training) that was going to ensure companies' success. Next it was psychological testing both for job applicants and for management development. Then it was MBO (management-by-objectives) and quantitative management. The 1960s brought matrix management, centralization/decentralization, statistical quality control, diversified conglomerates, sensitivity training, and the Managerial Grid. In the 1970s it was transactional analysis, quality circles, zero-based budgeting, strategic planning, portfolio management and SPC (statistical process control). The 1980s brought MBWA (management by walking around), the One-Minute-Manager, a new JIT (just-in-time provisioning), TQM (total quality management), restructuring, "intrapreneuring", focusing on shareholder value and changing corporate cultures. The 1990s brought us downsizing, de-layering, re-engineering and the learning organization. Since 2000 it's been outsourcing. All this adds up to a new "key" every 1.8 years!

This history would be comic if it were not also sad. It is comic to see the futile result of American management's insatiable lust for quick fixes. It is sad to see the waste of so many worthwhile ideas and approaches discarded and unused. Each of the above-listed twenty-six "keys" has value. But in order for this value to be realized, managements must first understand realistically the true potential and limitations of each new idea. They also must understand and be willing to do the work necessary to put the new idea to actual use.

Instead, each of these innovations was often "misconscrewed" by its proponents who promised far too much. There was more misconscrewing by managers whose expectations were unrealistically high, and who wanted to show by their actions, that they were doing *something*. They failed to understand and were unwilling to make the changes in the way they and their organizations had to behave in order to gain the promised benefits. They looked for quick fixes when in reality, major investments in time and effort were required. They believed that the *perception* of certain actions was more important than actually accomplishing anything. No wonder they were disappointed in the outcomes.

Some Important Lessons

What lessons can be drawn from this history and commentary? Are there no keys to success for organizations? Are the dual problems of defining success and achieving lasting changes so complicated and daunting that we should forget about trying and give up? Should we become much more cautious in taking up new ideas?

Certainly not! But in order to become more successful, managements must change attitudes and actions. They must become more clear and precise in defining what success means for their organizations. Only then can they improve the likelihood that they will actually achieve it.

Managements must also change mind-sets. They must drop any dreams about quick fixes and face up to the true nature of the problems they are tackling. They must understand the complexity of these problems and appreciate what it takes to resolve them on a continuing basis. In doing so, they will develop a broader, more useful notion of their role and what they can accomplish with and through their organizations. They will also understand how available but unused or discarded innovative ideas can be rehabilitated and put to constructive use.

This is what this book is about.

CHAPTER 2

WHAT IS TRUE SUCCESS?

Traditional ways of defining organizational success are faulty. One-dimensional, fixed definitions are insufficient and misleading. Any useful definition of success must take into account five facts.

1. Success is more a perception than an objective fact.

2. There are several groups, both within and outside any organization, whose perceptions matter; each has its own way of looking at and evaluating success.

3. Perceptions of success stem from both subjective considerations and objective indicators of organizational performance.

4. Criteria for defining success vary from business to not-for-profit to government organizations.

5. Criteria for defining success change over time.

The implications of these facts taken together are disturbing. Is true success definable only for a particular organization during a specific time period? Is it possible to formulate a broad general definition of success, valid for every organization?

Following Up A Prior Approach to Defining Success

Reconsider an important earlier effort to define success for corporations. In their best selling book, *In Search of Excellence*, T.J. Peters and R.H. Waterman, Jr. laid out in 1982 eight traits of "excellent", successful business organizations. The book was an outcome of a four-year study of 62 large U.S. corporations selected for their track record and reputation for excellence.

To test Peters' and Waterman's criteria for success, I followed up how 48 of these firms performed a decade and a half later in the mid-1990s and for the preceding decade (the other 14 were either privately held with no public information available, or had merged). I repeated this analysis in mid-2005. In Appendix A, I describe in detail the approaches used by Peters and Waterman in their initial study, and in my follow-ups, along with the results.

Of the 48 corporations initially characterized as "excellent" or successful in the early 1980s, only 40%would fit that characterization in the mid-l990s. Of the 36 firms followed up in mid-2005, fewer than 1/3 could be considered a superior performer. This raises a question about Peters' and Waterman's definition of success. Are their underlying criteria flawed?.

Reconsidering the Criteria

In my follow-up studies, I applied six criteria matching the ones used by Peters and Waterman. Four are factual and objective (total returns, earnings-per share growth, market value added (MVA), and improvement in MVA rank). All are financial, appropriate only for businesses. They are meaningless and irrelevant for not-for-profit and government organizations.

The other two criteria (customer satisfaction and company reputation) are subjective. They depend on perceptions by informed observers outside the organizations being evaluated. Unlike the objective criteria, these could be applied to not-for-profit and government organizations ... but only if the definitions of customer satisfaction and organizational reputation were modified. For any broad definition of organizational success, all six criteria have only limited value.

From my follow-up studies it appears that when assessing success for business organizations, perceptions outweigh objective financial performance criteria. When a list of companies with clearly superior objective performance measures is compared with a list of most admired firms, less than 40% appear in both lists. Clearly, company reputations are based on more than returns, MVA and earnings growth. There is a higher correlation, however, between the two subjective criteria: company reputation and customer satisfaction.

Conclusions From the Follow-Up

However relevant for businesses the criteria used in the early 1980s to define success might be, they cannot be used for other kinds of organizations. Nor are they sufficient for defining *consistent* long-term success, even for businesses.

Clearly, success today doesn't necessarily mean success tomorrow. Things change, both within companies, and in their external environments. Any organization's ability to perform consistently well over long periods of time depends on two factors. First, management must detect and anticipate changes that are relevant to the organization. Then the organization must appropriately adapt the way it works.

The global computer industry, is a useful laboratory for observing changes external to organizations and their ability to adapt. I have worked with the top managements of several leading firms in this industry over several decades.

Since the mid-1960s, this industry has experienced continuous revolutionary changes, driven largely by rapid technological developments in semiconductors. Replacing printed circuit boards, these tiny devices pack ever-increasing computing power and memory capacity in ever-shrinking space. One result has been vast increases in computing capability at radically lower costs. Another result has been a shift in focus on what is crucially important, from computing machines or "hardware" to operating and applications programs or "software". A third result has been a shift in customer concerns from technology and what it can do, to getting their business and organizational problems solved. Since 1980, these basic changes have been taking place simultaneously at an increasingly rapid pace.

During the 1990s and since, another technological revolution has been impacting the computer industry. The internet has vastly extended the capabilities and use of computers beyond self-contained machines that store and manipulate data, to communications terminals on the world-wide web of information and software. The internet has imposed on computers the need for entirely new functionalities.

Consider how the four leading firms in the industry (in the 1980s) have fared. Three, IBM, Digital Equipment Corporation (DEC), and Hewlett-Packard (H-P) were included in Peters' and Waterman's "exemplar" companies. The fourth, Apple, emerged in the 1980s as a powerhouse in personal computers, but then declined in the following decade, and recovered somewhat by 2004. In the early 1990s, all four of these industry leaders were experiencing serious performance problems. A decade later, DEC had been acquired by Compaq (later Compaq was acquired by H-P). By 2005, DEC had vanished and the other three firms were struggling to regain the stellar performance they exhibited in the 1980s.

All four companies sank into the doldrums for the same basic reason. All had trouble adapting to changes in the industry. Their difficulties stemmed from their earlier successes. These caused the enshrinement of values and work habits that strongly influenced decisions affecting organizational performance. For example, hardware designers wielded the strongest influence. Highest commitment was to products that accounted for the firms' early successes (large mainframes for IBM, minicomputers with proprietary software for DEC, personal computers with proprietary software for Apple). Convinced they knew what customers needed and wanted, engineers prevailed over marketers and salespeople when it came to designing products.

These attitudes and values drove peoples' behavior, forming the companies' cultures. Strengthened by each organization's early successes, they led to arrogance. Once formed, these cultures resisted change. Yet radical change was crucial for adapting to the changes in technology and customer needs that were occurring at bewildering speeds. A focus on hardware and commitment to products responsible for a company's initial success are incompatible with providing solutions to customers' business problems. It is not surprising that these proud companies foundered.

Further Facts About Success and Organizations

In rethinking how organizational success can be defined more broadly and usefully, consider the following additional facts about organizations and success.

1. Every organization, business, not-for-profit, or government, works to achieve objectives, either explicitly stated or implied.

2. Objectives set by an organization's leaders may reflect personal agendas but often take into account interests and concerns of other groups as well. These are both within the organization (employee groups in particular locations and categories, and union leaders), and outside (investment analysts, shareholders, outside directors, funders, and interested parties in the media and academia).

3. Objectives also take into consideration opportunities and constraints outside the organization, along with the organization's capabilities to achieve whatever it sets out to do.

4. Objectives change over time.

5. When an organization achieves its objectives consistently over time, it is and is seen as successful.

A New Definition of True Success for Organizations

In light of the above, a new, more useful definition of true success for organizations is needed. Ultimately, an organization's success is determined by how well over time it sets and achieves objectives. This way of thinking is applicable to any organization, business, not-for-profit and government.

Here, then, is my new definition:

True success for any organization is its ability to set appropriate objectives and then to achieve them consistently over time.

This definition is free of any absolute criteria such as customer satisfaction, growth, returns, productivity or profits. Rather, it is dynamic, allowing for changes in objectives over time. It accommodates the factors influencing objective setting, especially leaders' personal agendas. And it takes into account the difficulties of changing the way organizations work. Most important, this definition opens up for every organization new approaches for achieving true success.

In Chapter 4, I discuss in further detail, objectives, how they are set, and the notion of appropriateness.

CHAPTER 3

WHAT DETERMINES TRUE SUCCESS?

If an organization is truly successful when it consistently sets and achieves appropriate objectives, what does it take to accomplish this? To understand how an organization must behave in order to ensure success, we must look more deeply at the drivers or basic forces that determine true success. Then we can specify what organizations *need* to put in place if they are to be truly successful.

Four drivers combine to generate true success. The way they work together are shown in the Figure 1 model. Most fundamental is *understanding* what is currently going on and what future developments are likely to occur regarding key factors in an organization's external environment. It is equally important to understand what is going on within the organization itself ... which things are working well and which things are not. Understanding both the external and internal situations enables management to develop the second driver: *identification of potentially attractive opportunities* for the organization, along with any *warning signals*.

A third driver is *plans* that both target which opportunities to pursue and which warning signals to take seriously and address, and describe how best to accomplish all this. The quality of creative ideas determine how appropriate are the opportunities and warning signals identified, along with the plans to deal with them. The fourth driver is *organizational focus* ... key to the successful pursuit of selected opportunities and address of serious warning signals. Focus includes continuous monitoring of both the organization's external environment, and of how effectively the organization itself is performing. This ensures that management's *understanding* continues to be current, comprehensive and accurate.

Identifying and Defining An Organization's Business(es)

In our model (<u>Drivers for True Success</u>, Figure 1), all four drivers depend on knowing what is going on both outside and inside the organization. To set appropriate objectives for an organization, management need *relevant information* both about the external environment and the way things are working internally. This is as true for not-for-profit and governmental organizations as is it for businesses. When such information is interpreted in a particular context, knowledge and understanding result. Management needs to know where to look for information, what data to gather and how these should be interpreted. <u>*Relevant information about the organization and its external environment is fundamental to achieving true success.*</u>

The amount of external and internal information is limitless. To make this task manageable requires determining which information is relevant. It also requires focusing how information is gathered.

A key starting point for any organization is to identify and define each "business" it is conducting. This not only determines the scope for both external and internal information gathering, but also provides the context for relevance (see <u>Gathering Information</u>, Figure 2).

By "business" I mean a related set of activities conducted within the organization to produce offerings for the marketplace (products and/or services) targeted to a defined set of customers. Thus, businesses are conducted not only by for-profit organizations, but also by not-for-profit and government organizations.

> For example, a school is in the business of offering to a defined age group of students in a defined geographic area, services intended to develop their skills and capabilities to prepare them for higher education, or careers, or specific work, paid or unpaid. Museums, libraries and historical societies are all in business of collecting, storing, preserving and exhibiting artifacts for purposes of research, education and entertainment. Human services agencies are in the business of offering specific services (e.g. adoption, individual and family counseling, help with gaining employment, housing, counseling for addiction, etc.) to population segments within a community characterized by special needs (e.g. mental retardation, disabilities, barriers to employment, substance addiction, homelessness, etc.).

Figure 1
DRIVERS FOR TRUE SUCCESS: A MODEL

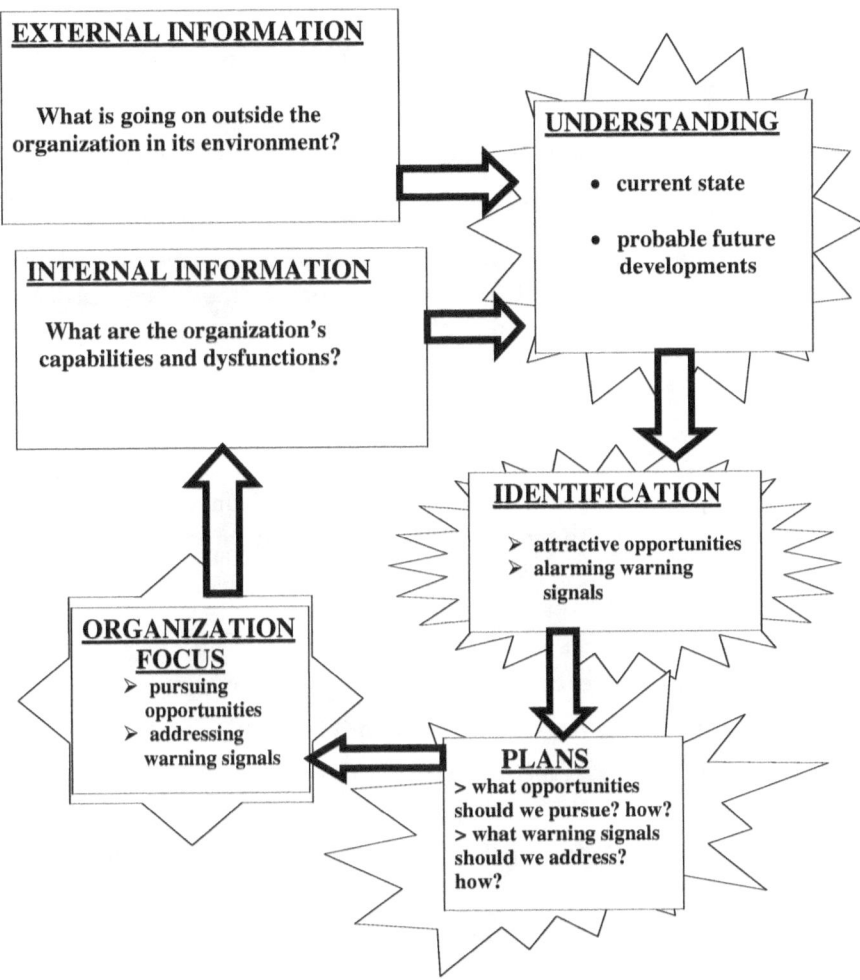

Most organizations carry on only a single business. Some however, conduct two or more businesses. These may be related or distinctly different. Identifying the number of businesses an organization is conducting and defining each of these are fundamental prerequisites for an organization seeking true success. Answering these questions is more art than science (1). Nevertheless management must do so in order to determine the scope, focus and context for both external and internal information.

Three criteria help determine whether a business is truly distinct, or part of some other business in the organization (the term Strategic Business Unit or SBU is often used):

1. Its mission/strategic intent (2) differs from the mission of any other business in the organization.

2.It participates or competes in an external market with distinct sets of customers, rivals, sources of revenue and distribution channels.

3. It must be able to formulate and implement strategic plans with relatively little impact on or from other businesses in the organization. These plans deal with products and services, sources of revenue, markets, prices, facilities and organization.

All three clues for deciding how a potential "business" meets these criteria are external to the organization. If most of the following seven questions can be answered with "yes", then the business is most likely distinct. If not, then the business is probably part of some other business in the organization:

For any potentially distinct business:

- Do its customers differ from those of the organization's other businesses?
- Do its competitors differ from those of the organization's other businesses?
- Do its distribution channels differ from those of the organization's other businesses?
- Do its sources of revenue differ from those of the organization's other businesses?
- Can it price its offerings without concern for how this will impact the organization's other businesses?
- Can it make decisions about the quality and style of its offerings without concern for how this will impact the organization's other businesses?
- Can it be divested or liquidated without adversely impacting other businesses in the organization?

Figure 2
GATHERING INFORMATION

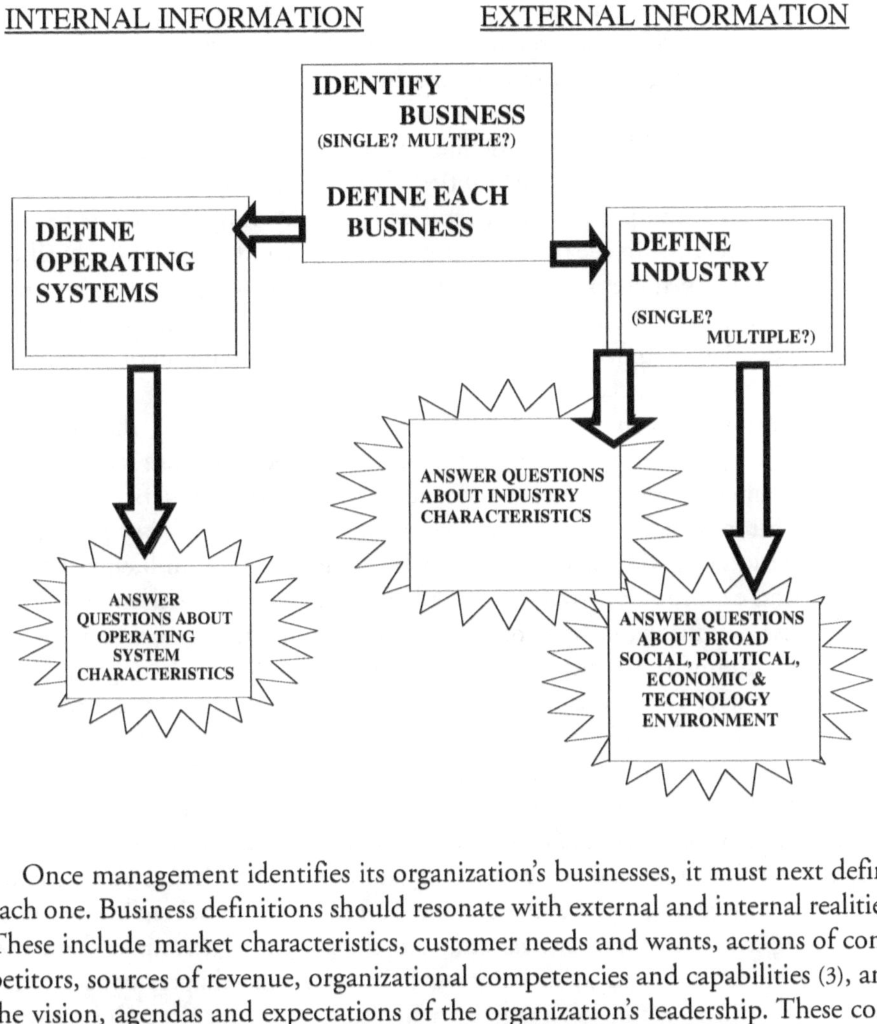

INTERNAL INFORMATION   EXTERNAL INFORMATION

```
            IDENTIFY
               BUSINESS
            (SINGLE? MULTIPLE?)

            DEFINE EACH
DEFINE  ⇐   BUSINESS          ⇒  DEFINE
OPERATING                        INDUSTRY
SYSTEMS                          (SINGLE?
                                     MULTIPLE?)
```

ANSWER QUESTIONS ABOUT INDUSTRY CHARACTERISTICS

ANSWER QUESTIONS ABOUT OPERATING SYSTEM CHARACTERISTICS

ANSWER QUESTIONS ABOUT BROAD SOCIAL, POLITICAL, ECONOMIC & TECHNOLOGY ENVIRONMENT

Once management identifies its organization's businesses, it must next define each one. Business definitions should resonate with external and internal realities. These include market characteristics, customer needs and wants, actions of competitors, sources of revenue, organizational competencies and capabilities (3), and the vision, agendas and expectations of the organization's leadership. These considerations change over time. No business definition can be regarded as fixed. It must be reviewed periodically and revised when appropriate.

For 57 years, the Celebrity Series of Boston, a major arts organization, defined its business as presenting to Boston audiences "the very best in music, dance and performing arts from around the world". A typical season would consist of 40–50 concerts, dance and other per-

forming arts programs. Faced with a declining number of subscribers
and a fall-off of ticket sales for individual events, management revised
the business definition. The new definition retained the traditional one,
but added the concept of building new audiences for the future. To
implement this, the organization now offers an extensive educational
outreach program to attract young people.

Two issues need addressing to define an organization's business(es). One is
ensuring that the definition fits the realities of the organization's markets and customers along with the products and services it is delivering. The other issue is
ensuring that everyone in the organization understands and supports the business
definition(s). When there is lack of clarity or differences of opinion about business definitions, it is difficult to achieve and sustain focus within the organization
on objectives, plans and priorities. This can seriously undermine an organization's
ability to achieve true success.

Both these issues can be resolved when management makes the effort to
address them explicitly (unfortunately, this seldom happens because management
takes for granted that everyone understands and buys in). Understanding and
agreement can readily be achieved first by assembling a group of "key players" in
the organization (individuals with the knowledge and power to influence the formulation and execution of strategies and plans), and then after debating alternative business definitions in light of information about the organization and its
external environment, reaching consensus. My term for such a group is a
Planning Group (PG). This can number from 10–40 members, and is key to the
SONG process discussed in detail in Chapter 6.

Once agreement is reached on a business definition, this must then be communicated, along with the underlying rationale, throughout the organization.
Review, examination, debate and agreement on business definitions should occur
at regular intervals (annually or bi-annually) to ensure that definitions are congruent with any changes within the organization and its external environment.

Defining a business is a critical strategic choice. Recall examples from the
computer industry described in Chapter 2. Later in this chapter consider the
changes in business definition made by a British beer company, and a regional
insurance provider of low denomination insurance for death and funeral costs.

Understanding the External Environment

When gathering information about an organization's external environment,
attention should be directed to general forces and trends in two domains. One is

the relevant geographical area (community, metropolitan area, state or province, region, nation, continent, world). The other is the "industry" in which each of the organization's businesses participates.

Defining an Industry

Gathering external information should begin within the "industry" of which a business is part. An industry is made up of businesses/organizations within a specified geographic area providing related products and services intended for a common market. Some of these businesses compete with one another for customers or clients or other revenue sources. Others such as partners, suppliers and distributors, collaborate. Industries can be local, regional, national, international or global. Just as defining an organization's business(es) is more art than science, so too is defining its industry. This is neither an obvious nor trivial task.

From the outset, anyone seeking industry knowledge is confronted with a dilemma. An organization needs to understand what is going on in the industry in order to identify possible opportunities and warning signals. The scope for defining that industry must not be narrowly focused. Yet, the industry definition cannot be so broad that it resists relevant analysis. The following examples may help illuminate a useful approach to industry definition.

Here are five examples of industry definitions that were too narrowly focused.

A U.S. manufacturer of dry swimming pool chemicals defined its industry as U.S. dry swimming pool chemicals. Management wanted to ignore the fact that more than 90% of swimming pool chemicals sold in the U.S. was liquid chlorine. The firm thus claimed a leading share of the market. By defining the industry narrowly, management was constrained in its thinking and efforts to convert customers using liquid chlorine to dry product ... by far its best opportunity to grow the business dramatically.

A U.S. producer of industrial process measurement instruments and controls identified its industry as North American process instruments. Management missed the fact that both the market for and providers of process control instruments had become global. Competitors were thinking and acting beyond national boundaries, leaving the U.S. firm in their wake.

A social agency providing rehabilitation services for the emotionally disabled in a major northeastern U.S. city saw its industry as emotional disability rehabilitation in that city. But the social agency was attracting clients from outside the city. Many had physical and mental disabilities in addition to emotional problems. The agency was actually participating in an industry that was regional, not local, encompassing a broader range of disabilities than emotional ones. A broader industry definition facilitated understanding and analysis of competing programs and alternative sources of clients and funding.

In the U.S., a mid-western state's Department of Transportation determined that it was part of the U.S. Transportation industry. The Department was concerned in part with a major international airport and marine terminal on Lake Michigan. By broadening their industry definition from national to global, policy makers and administrators were able to take a wider view of competing ports of entry as well as developments in technology and policy.

A major London art museum decided that it was part of the British fine arts exhibition industry. By defining its industry as national, the London art museum missed two facts: not only was the art market global, so too were opportunities to mount traveling "blockbuster" exhibitions as ways to enhance revenues.

Here is an example of too broad an industry definition

A brokerage firm providing supporting services to financial advisers throughout the U.S. believed it was part of the U.S. financial services industry. The firm's definition of its industry included not only all kinds of brokerage firms, but also insurance companies, banks, other savings and loan institutions, finance companies, mutual funds and the like. Such a scope was too broad and complex to be useful. After considerable study, the firm's leaders decided to focus primarily on a *sub-segment* of the brokerage segment of the U.S. financial services industry, Financial Advisor Services

Here are two industry definitions that were initially off the mark strategically.

A regional provider of insurance sold through funeral homes in the southeastern U.S. to cover funeral expenses defined its industry as low-denomination insurance sold in the southeast. The insurer was aware of several rapidly growing trends in the North American death industry that were eroding its business. One trend was the entry into this stable, unsophisticated, tradition-ridden industry of more than 22,000 family-owned funeral homes, of several large strategically sophisticated corporations. Through acquisition, they were establishing chains of funeral homes with strong purchasing power, able to provide fully integrated services. The fastest growing service was an innovation called "pre-need" planning in which an individual while still living could specify in detail with the help of a counselor, all aspects of his or her desired burial arrangements, rites, etc., and fund this with a new kind of "pre-need" insurance. To defend themselves from takeover, independent funeral homes also began offering pre-need counseling and insurance.

The regional insurer's management decided to redefine its business to capitalize on the opportunities presented by the rapid development of pre-need. It shifted its focus away from providing small denomination insurance policies for death costs to individuals through funeral homes. Instead, the firm wanted to become a provider to funeral directors of a sophisticated integrated package of services designed to help them enter and succeed in the pre-need business. This package included computer-driven business planning and lead management tools, selection and training of pre-need counselors, and of course, pre-need insurance. The corresponding industry was redefined as pre-need services.

A top U.K. beer company defined itself as a participant in the British beer industry. Management assumed it was in the beer business until a strategy consultant pointed out that 1300 company-owned pubs in prime urban locations had a much greater asset value than the firm's three breweries. Furthermore beer drinking was only one of several activities in these pubs, ranking fourth in importance in the customer's choice of pub and in the pub's revenues ... after gaming machines, entertainment and food. After much debate, management decided that it was really in the business of leisure time use. Accordingly, it redefined its industry as leisure time activities. This repositioning had a profound, dramatically positive impact on the firm's strategy and subsequent performance.

These examples show that how an organization defines each business and relevant industry is a critical strategic choice. If the scope is too narrowly focused, management myopia (4) is likely to result and thus constrain the organization's future development and performance. If the scope is too broad, management will have difficulty making sense of its external world. If the scope fails to reflect market and competitive changes requiring the organization to rethink and redefine its business, the result may be stagnation or decline.

Industry Information

In gathering information about an industry, here are the key questions to be answered:

- **Size:** Current size of the industry (total aggregate revenues and investments for businesses; aggregate budgets for governmental and not-for-profit organizations)? Changes in size in the past 5–10 years; changes projected for next 5–10 years?

- **Number of Participants:** How many organizations in the industry? How have numbers changed in past 5–10 years; projected change in next 5–10 years?

- **Principal Organizations:** What organizations account for most revenues, sources of funds, investments or budgets in industry as a whole? Ranking by size, market or budget share? Changes in rankings in past 5–10 years? Nature and history of principal organizations? What does each offer to what markets and segments? Strengths, weaknesses, strategies and customer/public perceptions of each organization?

- **Markets Served:** Characteristics of market(s) and market segments served? Basis of market segmentation? Who are customers, clients or users and what are their characteristics and needs? What is the market potential?

- **Market Offerings:** What are principal market offerings (goods, services)? Variety in market offerings? Increasing, stable or decreasing? How well established is concept and design of offerings? How are these distributed to customers, clients and users? How are these promoted, advertised and sold? Criteria determining customer/user choice? Importance of brand, trademark and reputation in determining choice

- **Pricing:** How are market offerings priced (historical, actual and potential)? Opportunities for price differentiation? How flexible is pricing?

- **Competitive Dynamics:** Nature and bases of competition (for customers, funders)? Competitive "games" played? What constitutes competitive advantage and disadvantage?

- **Industry Economics:** Characteristics of industry economics? Capital, labor intensity? How are costs structured? What are typical returns, profitability and cash flow? Seasonality and/or cyclicality? How easy or difficult is it to enter this industry? How are organizations funded? From what sources?

- **Innovation:** Role played by innovation? Importance? Typical life-cycles of market offerings? Nature, importance and cost of research and development?

- **Technology:** Nature of and role of technology (for facilities, operating equipment and processes, systems, tooling, information)? Crucial skills and know-how?

- **Operations:** Nature of and role of operations? How standardized? How flexible? Mass processing or short, tailored production runs? Priorities for quality, cost, delivery, reliability and flexibility?

- **Legislation, Regulations, Unions:** Nature of and role of legislation, regulation and trade unions? Importance and impact?

In seeking answers to these questions about industry characteristics and dynamics, special attention should be paid to past and probable future changes and trends.

As an example of information about an industry, consider software in the U.S.

Less than 50 years old, this high growth industry is comprised of hundreds of firms, most small. The giant Microsoft is dominant, but innovation, ease of entry and very rapid technological change (most recently, the Internet) enable any group of clever software designers to establish an initial foothold in one or more of the industry's many niche markets.

Becoming successful is more difficult. The software industry operates on the economic principle of "increasing returns" (5). This means that whichever firm gains the lead in a market, it can get further ahead. Winners clean up; losers are wiped out. The reason: the software business has high fixed costs (mostly up-front research and development ... costs of raw material, inventory and manufacturing plant and equipment are very low), and low variable costs. As volume rises, per unit costs plummet. Gross margins often reach 90% ... the more units sold, the greater the profit. Production cost per unit shipped is comparatively low. When the Internet is the distribution channel, production cost per unit is negligible. Even tiny firms can produce unlimited amounts of software. According to Bill Gurley, a director at the DMG Technology Group of Deutsche Morgan Grenfell, "Never in the history of the industrialized world has there been a business that has the advantages of scale of the software industry."

With this leverage of fixed costs, the industry's volume leader in a market segment can use price to gain further competitive advantage. When the market leader cuts price, the reduction to profits and returns is modest because these are already very high due to huge volume. For weaker competitors with relatively low volumes, responsive price cuts often force them into a loss position. This causes considerable churn in firms entering and leaving the industry.

Thus, market share is critical. Once a firm has established itself, a reliable stream of recurring revenue can be ensured from selling software upgrades to its existing customers. There is a further competitive advantage for market leaders: the more widely used a particular piece of software, the more it is valued. Other software is designed and sold to work with it. This, in turn, further enhances its value.

Another industry characteristic is that once customers have made the investment to master a particular piece of software, there is a big incentive to stay with it. It may not be worth the cost of switching to a different product, even if it has some better features. For an established product to be dislodged, the alternative would have to be dramatically better. Yet there is a reluctance to be first in adopting a new technology. This can be offset somewhat when perceived, respected leaders in the user community are enthusiastic in their support of a new technology.

Information About the Broader External Environment

Beyond understanding what is going in its industry, management also needs to be aware of relevant trends in the broader economic, political, social and technological forces that impact its organization. Information about these forces should focus on past and probable future changes and trends. The scope for answering questions such as the following should correspond to the industry's geographical scope (local, regional, national, international or global):

-   **Economic Trends:** What is happening with key elements of the economy (inflation, interest rates, exchange rates, employment, wealth distribution, financial markets, balance of payments, national debt, international trade, etc.)?

-   **Political Trends:** What is happening in the political arena (changes in government policy and leadership, political issues, conflicts and alliances, legislation and regulation, government programs, minority interests and concerns, political pressure groups, etc.)?

- <u>Social Trends:</u> Significant social issues and trends? Demographic changes and implications? Shifting social agendas and changing needs of population segments? Power and agenda of organized labor? Implications of changing work force demographics? Adequacy of education and training to meet required knowledge and skills?

- <u>Technological Trends:</u> What is direction of developments in technology, especially in materials, communication, information and robotics?

Understanding the Internal Environment

Along with understanding major changes and trends in an organization's external environment, management also needs a comprehensive, realistic view of its organization's internal characteristics. It needs a clear grasp of its organization's key competencies, capabilities, strengths, weaknesses and culture (6). Understanding these in concert with relevant external developments is necessary to identify possible opportunities for the organization along with warning signals.

An organization's competencies, capabilities, strengths, weaknesses and culture are key to what it is good at doing and accomplishing. These are also key to what an organization is *not* good at doing. Some weaknesses and cultural beliefs and norms are potential obstacles for an organization if it is to change in certain desired ways. Recall the examples in Chapter 2 of the computer companies unable to abandon their focus on engineering design and hardware, the bases for their earlier success.

Determining Scope: Defining An Operating System

As with external information, there is a prior issue of scope to be resolved in gathering internal information, especially in larger, more complex organizations. Here, the focus should be on those parts of the organization that work together to support each distinct business.

Once management has determined and defined each business in the organization, it must answer another question before clarifying the scope for gathering internal information: what operating *system or systems* support each business (7)? Carrying on a business requires coordinating and integrating several organizational elements. These include those organizational functions, departments and business processes that support a business along with all the people, systems and policies and procedures associated with these functions and processes.

Here are some examples of business processes ... all the activities required to:

-   develop a new product or service and bring it to market;
-   take, process and fill customer orders;
-   procure and pay for materials, components and supplies.

An operating system is the combination of functions, business processes, people, systems, and policies and procedures. Internal information is about operating systems ... describing them and how they work, so that competencies, capabilities, dysfunctions and system performance can be identified and assessed.

As with identifying and defining businesses and industries, defining operating systems is more art than science. Three different criteria must be considered. An operating system should support only one business, not two or more. An operating system should be truly systemic ... encompassing many functions and cross-functional business processes. And an operating system should be manageable when efforts are made to change and improve the way it performs. This means it should not be so large and complex that the barriers to change are intimidating.

A useful starting point for defining an operating system is a physical facility. This is because every sizable facility has a unique history and culture. Depending on the situation, there are alternative approaches to defining operating systems. The simplest case is an organization of fewer than 1000 employees conducting a single business within one facility. In this instance, the operating system is the entire organization. All three of the above criteria are satisfied.

When an organization conducting a single business is very large, with many facilities in different locations, several operating systems are involved. Each centers on a major (sizeable) facility (A) and includes all the functions, business processes, people, systems, and policies and procedures in A. In addition, key functions, business processes, people, etc. in the head office which influence and impact A's performance would also be part of that operating system, along with other facilities that frequently interact with A. When several major facilities work together to support a single business, differences among them warrant the definition of separate operating systems, as illustrated in the following example.

A U.S. producer of large truck axles had three manufacturing plants in addition to a separate head office facility. Forgings were made by 600 unionized employees in an old plant in Ohio. The equipment was aging and not well maintained. Relations between the union and management were hostile. Productivity was low. The forgings were machined in a plant in Indiana 400 miles distant, by 1200 unionized employees. This factory, too, was old, but the equipment was well maintained. Union-management relations were generally positive. But productivity suffered because of poor control over the flow of materials from the forging plant and from many other suppliers, and within the plant itself. The axles were assembled by 1800 non-unionized employees in a new South Carolina plant. In this facility management was applying a variety of "new" approaches such as total quality management, flat organizational structures and employee empowerment. Productivity was high. All three plants were controlled from a head office in Michigan where the axles were designed and marketed. There also resided the functions of sales and services management, finance and administration, human resources and labor relations, legal, and information services and technology.

Management decided that three operating systems were supporting their business. Each centered on one of the manufacturing facilities, but included those functions in head office that influenced plant performance along with relevant functions in those other plants that supplied components. Three operating systems were specified because the circumstances, histories and problems of each facility were so different from those of the others. By defining each operating system to include head office and supply sources, management ensured a truly systemic scope.

In single businesses with many small facilities (for example, fast food or retail chains), no single facility is large enough to warrant definition as a distinct operating system. In such instances, an operating system can be based on a geographical region. This system would include all the facilities in the region, appropriate head office functions and the relevant warehousing facility. This approach works because the individual facilities are typically more alike than different with regard to technology and business processes. Differences in customer needs and tastes and in employee characteristics are more likely to be regional than local.

In very large organizations that carry on several different businesses, seldom does a facility support only a single business. This is also true of functional departments. In such instances, each operating system contains all functions, activities and business processes that support or supply a single business, *wherever they are located in the organization*. Relevant supporting systems, policies and procedures are also included.

A large functional department providing supporting services throughout the organization (human resources, information technology and services, finance, etc.) could also be defined as an operating system provided that the scope of that system extends beyond the function's boundaries. Thus, in addition to all key departments and activities within the function itself, the operating system needs to include key internal customers and suppliers, and related "sister" functions along with associated business processes, systems, policies and procedures.

Internal Information

In gathering information about an operating system, here are the key questions to be answered:

- **Scope:** What is the operating system's scope ... which functions, work flows, business processes, systems, policies and procedures are included? Relation of operating system to rest of organization? Key services supporting operating system from elsewhere in organization? Demands made on system by other businesses and support functions in organization?

- **Structure:** What is the organizational structure within operating system (matrix, functional, divisional, etc.)? Number of levels? Geographic aspects?

- **Management:** What management characteristics predominate? Age and tenure of senior and middle-level managers? Education and experience? Management style and behavior? Perceived priorities? Ratio of managers to those managed? How is time allocated and applied?

- **Inter functional Activity:** What is nature and extent of cross-functional interaction and collaboration?

- **First Line Supervision:** Characteristics of first-line supervision? Age and tenure? Education and experience? Ratio of supervisors to those supervised? How is time allocated and applied? Supervisory style and behavior?

- **Workforce:** Characteristics of work force? Age and seniority distribution? Employees by job category and function? Levels of skill and competence? Changes/trends in nature of work force?

- **Training:** Nature of training and development? Needs/activities? Investment? Career movement?

- **Climate:** Characteristics of work climate? Motivators/demotivators? Morale level/trends?

- **Planning:** Nature of planning and scheduling? Long-term strategic planning? Shorter-term tactical planning and scheduling? Materials control?

- **Management Information:** Characteristics of management information within operating system and between it and other organizational units? Quality, relevance, timeliness and effectiveness for decision support? Supporting systems? Automation?

- **Performance Measures:** Controls and performance measures in use? What is measured and controlled? Nature of measures and controls? Alignment with strategy? Alignment among business, operating system and departmental levels? Behavior encouraged?

- **Communications:** Nature of communications within operating system and between it and other organizational units? Content? Mechanisms used? Characteristics (top-> down, bottom->up, lateral)? Effectiveness?

- **Rewards:** Rewards and compensation used? Characteristics of compensation system structure? Comparative levels ... internal and external? Relation to performance? Non-monetary rewards and recognition?

- **Facilities and Equipment:** Characteristics of physical facilities and equipment? Age and condition? Attractiveness? Maintenance? Mechanization and automation?

- **Performance:** Characteristics of operating system's performance? Actual vs. objectives and priorities? How are customer satisfaction, flexibility and productivity measured? Recent trends in measured results?

- **Culture:** Predominant characteristics of operating system's culture? Beliefs that influence decision choices? Norms that influence behavior?

Developing an Information Database

The quality of information depends on the quality of the database describing the organization and its external environment. This database provides management with everything it needs to know in order to develop the understanding it needs to identify attractive opportunities, threats and plans.

A high quality database can be developed in at least 3 different ways. Each has its advantages and disadvantages. All three approaches require someone to lead the effort. This individual can be from within the organization or an outside consultant. In either case, that information database person (IDP) should meet the following criteria:

> ➤ broad understanding/knowledge of industry, market, competitor, funder and customer characteristics and dynamics
> ➤ broad knowledge/understanding of influential forces in the external environment … political, social, legislative, economic, technological, cultural
> ➤ broad understanding of organizational system dynamics
> ➤ knowledge and skills in research techniques … interviewing, internet, business data retrieval and analysis
> ➤ generally objective, independent outlook, free of bias

Real Time Development

In this approach to database development, the IDP assembles a group of knowledgeable members of the organization (or the PG) and interrogates them in a group session, following a checklist of topics and recording responses on flip charts for all to see and validate or revise. Such a session might take a full day.

Advantages: relatively little time and effort by the IDP; all participants learn and share; opportunity for questions, discussion and learning

Disadvantages: quality of information is constrained by limitations of knowledge and bias within the group; information is often subjective and incomplete; process is tedious and time-consuming for participants

"Fact Book"

The IDP prepares and distributes written questionnaires to appropriate members of management and technical specialists in the organization. From the responses, the IDP develops a "Fact Book" that describes the organization and its external environment. This book is then reviewed and agreed to individually by key members of management.

Advantages: relatively little time and effort by the IDP

Disadvantages: quality of information constrained by limitations of knowledge and bias within the organization; often subjective and incomplete; no assurance that every PG member will read and absorb the information; no opportunity for questions and discussion

Research and Preparation by IDP

IDP interviews key members of the organization and selected external stakeholders (funders, associations, government agencies, clients, etc.), collects and studies documents about the organization and its external environment, and does research on the internet. IDP develops a "straw person" description of the organization and its external environment for validation and modification by the PG in its initial work session. This straw description is best formatted in discrete statements of fact or perception, each dealing with a single topic, omitting any interpretation or suggestions of relationship or causality. Typically, any organization and its external environment can be described in 50–100 such statements. These are presented for discussion and validation/modification by the PG.

Ground rules for discussion are as follows: any statement of fact can be challenged; if after several minutes discussion of the challenged statement it cannot be modified to everyone's satisfaction, the statement is discarded; statements of perception can be discussed but not modified and discarded (a perception may be wrong, but if it exists, it is part of the reality and must be dealt with). The objectives for this discussion are for the PG to: (1) *understand comprehensively* what is going on both within and outside the organization; and (2) to *believe* the data. There are two ways in which the statements can be presented to the PG. One is a series of flip charts organized by topic categories. The other is a deck of 3X5 cards arranged randomly. I have found the latter to be more effective (see the discussion of process in strategic plan formulation in Chapter 6).

Advantages: database is comprehensive and relatively objective; the entire PG learns, understands and ends up owning the data; process is engaging and fun

Disadvantages: substantial time and work for the IDP

Understanding = Information + Meaning

Once the above questions are answered, management has a comprehensive overview of the past and current situation both internally and externally. This information however, is in the form of descriptive facts and perceptions. In order for these to be useful, they must be converted into understanding.

To transform information into understanding, it has to be invested with *meaning*. Facts and perceptions become meaningful when viewed in specific contexts such as the business' characteristics, organizational capabilities and management's objectives. Meaning also stems from assumptions about future developments based on past trends. Inevitably, management will perceive some facts and perceptions as *compelling* or especially significant. For example, in our description of the software industry earlier in this chapter, the criticality of market share is a compelling fact. These compelling facts and perceptions form the basis of management's understanding of its external environment and internal situation.

Three considerations provide the context for viewing and interpreting external and internal facts and perceptions. One is the business definition. Another is the aspirations of the organization's leaders. Third is the organization's competencies, capabilities and weaknesses. An identical set of facts about an industry will mean opportunity for some organizations, and warning signals to others.

Consider for example, North America's leading paint manufacturer. The North American paint industry has some atypical characteristics for an industry almost two centuries old. Despite its age, the industry continues to grow modestly in total revenues. Principal markets are new and refurbished construction (residential and industrial) and automotive. There are nearly a thousand competitors (declined from almost 1500 in the past 50 years), most of them local and regional. With such a high degree of fragmentation the leading firm's share of market is less than 7%. Paint technology and manufacturing processes are well and broadly understood. It has become increasingly difficult for customers to distinguish differences in paint quality from one supplier to another. Paint today is essentially a commodity, with price the foremost consideration in the decision to purchase. Service and special relationships also influence the purchase decision.

To our industry leader this set of facts about the industry was disturbing. Management wanted to increase sales and profits, turning around a steady erosion of both. It was counting on its traditional "strengths" of national distribution, high quality product and respected brand image. But the company was suffering from excess capacity in its many plants. Its "strengths" were offset by prices substantially higher than most competitors. In a commodity market the company's "strengths" had lost their value.

To a smaller regional paint manufacturer, the identical set of industry facts would appear promising. With a fully loaded plant, paint of adequate quality, low prices, strong customer relationships and reputation, and excellent service, a smaller, more nimble competitor would be well positioned to take business away from larger, more bureaucratic national suppliers. Furthermore, such a firm's management would probably set more modest profit and growth objectives than those of the market leader.

How significant is a past trend in an industry or in the broader external environment? The answer hinges on two considerations. One is how important the trending factor is in the context of the organization's circumstances. The other is the probability that the trend will continue. Forecasting the future is a risky business. But the risk can be lessened when alternative assumptions are made about future developments and their implications are thought through and made explicit. This approach is part of an organizational guidance and control system and process, and is discussed further in Chapter 6 in the section dealing with scenarios.

Identifying Opportunities and Warning Signals

Once management understands what is going on within its organization and its external environment it can identify *potentially attractive opportunities and warning signals*. This second driver for true success is most effectively accomplished by coupling a rigorous and regular application of a two-stage systematic process (see Figure 3, Identifying Attractive Opportunities and Warning Signals) with creative thinking.

The inputs that feed this process are the compelling facts and perceptions developed from information about the industry, the broader external environment and the operating system. In Stage 1 of this process, a small group of managers considers these in light of the business definition, aspirations of the organization's leaders, and the organization's capabilities, competencies and weaknesses. A number of potential opportunities and warning signals can then be identified. This task requires the ability to integrate and apply a wide range of information. It also requires creative imagination and thought. The processes and work required for an organization to generate and refine creative ideas are part of an organizational guidance and control system and process, discussed in Chapter 6.

The raw list of potential opportunities and warning signals must then be converted into a much shorter prioritized list of *attractive* opportunities and *alarming* warning signals. A set of screening criteria must be developed to test each potential opportunity and warning signal (Stage 2). These criteria form a gate through which a potential opportunity or warning signal must pass if it is to be judged truly attractive or alarming.

Some criteria are quantitative. Here are some examples: an attractive opportunity should yield no less than certain specified revenues, returns and/or profitability within a specified time period; the opportunity should require no more than a specified maximum level of resources to be fully realized; for a warning signal to be alarming, it could reduce revenues, market share and/or profitability by certain specified amounts.

Figure 3

<u>IDENTIFYING ATTRACTIVE OPPORTUNITIES AND ALARMING WARNING SIGNALS</u>

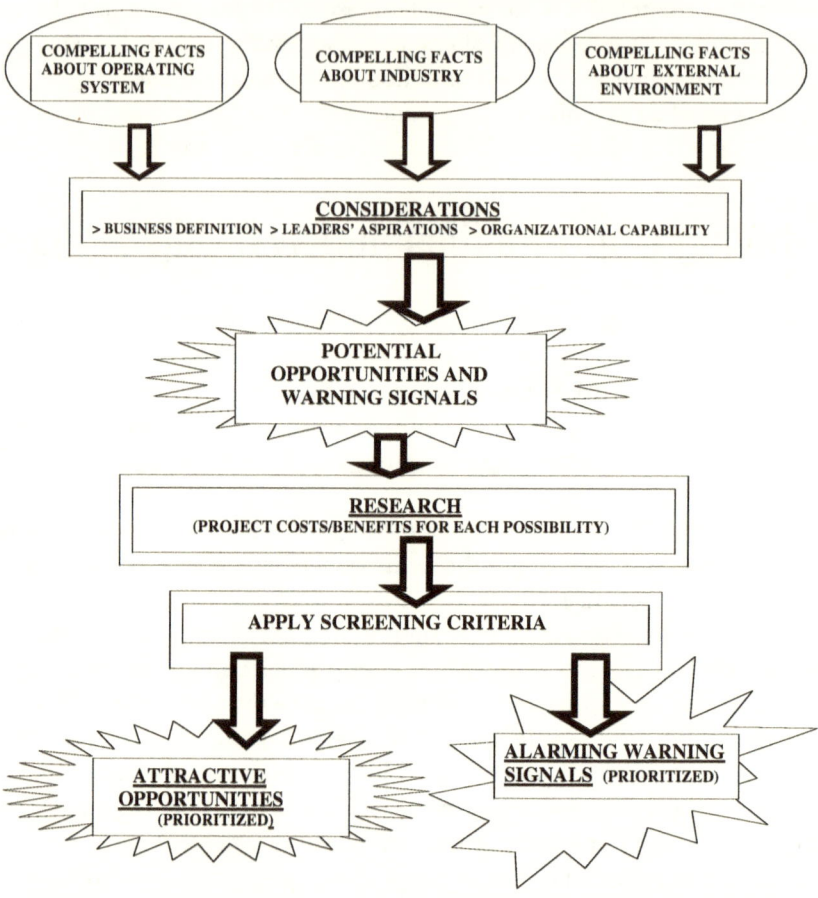

Other criteria are qualitative. For example: a true opportunity must be compatible with the organization's culture; environmental risk must not be increased; the organization's image and reputation must not suffer; the opportunity should fit the organization's mission and strategy; the existing business should not be undermined.

Before these criteria are applied, research is needed to answer the questions posed. For each potential opportunity, a projected cost/benefit analysis is required to resolve how well it meets not only the quantitative but also the qualitative criteria. Similarly, for each likely warning signal, estimates must be made of what might be impacted and to what extent. This research is also the basis for prioritizing the screened list of attractive opportunities and alarming warning signals.

Creative Thinking

The above process depends on creative thinking. Everyone is capable of this. This is apparent from children's play, especially the way they use art and construction materials. But as children grow to adults, their spontaneity and freedom of expression become inhibited. They learn that it is dangerous to voice creative thoughts because this might incur criticism and ridicule. In time, creativity gets suppressed. It takes a particular kind of supportive environment to rekindle people's creative spark.

This environment must provide stimulation. It must provide a context or framework of direction, guidelines and constraints. It must provide sufficient time (each work session should be at least a half-day). And the participants must feel safe to take risks in voicing their ideas, however undeveloped these might be.

The creative identification of potential opportunities and threats for an organization is most effectively done by a small group of no more than 5–6 managers selected for their broad understanding of the business and their track record for contributing good ideas and making sound decisions. Creative work is more easily done in the relatively comfortable, less intimidating environment of a small group. Each member should represent a different function. This ensures differences in perspective that provide stimulation.

The group should use a process that stimulates and supports creative thinking. The context should be made explicit at the outset. This includes the business definition, organizational and business strategic intent and objectives, strategic plan, cultural values, and organizational capabilities, competencies and weaknesses. Creative ideas are often more readily generated when direction and constraints are clear. For example, the composer Igor Stravinsky often set up arbitrary constraints for himself when he was composing (e.g. a core motif would be restricted to 7 notes, only 2 of which could be repeated). Group "brainstorming" techniques are useful and appropriate. These include making a deliberate effort at the outset to focus on idea generation, postponing critical assessment of each idea until a later phase. At first, each member of the group applies his/her energy towards accessing subjective thoughts and feelings, free-associating to one another's verbalizations and building on each other's ideas. These are recorded with no attempt to assess or critique their merit. Evaluation and selection by the group is done later on after everyone is satisfied that sufficient ideas have been generated (8).

Applying screening criteria to potential opportunities and threats (Stage 2) is a task that can readily be performed by a management group larger than the one designated (in Stage 1) to do the creative work needed to formulate the initial list of potential opportunities and threats. The kind of analytical and critical work needed to consider and screen possibilities is well suited to larger management groups (of up to 25–30 members). So too is the task of prioritizing the screened opportunities in order of attractiveness, and the screened threats in order of danger. Involving many managers rather than few has the benefit of improving the quality of the judgments made. Also, those involved develop understanding of the opportunities, what it will take to realize these, the risks and probable benefits. They also understand the threats, their possible impacts and implications. Those involved will also more likely be committed to carrying out whatever work is necessary to realize the opportunities and ward off the threats. In later chapters of this book, I suggest that such large groups of managers participate in formulating strategic and operating plans, and in monitoring their execution.

Determining What To Do About Selected Opportunities and Warning Signals

A third driver for true success is *plans* that embody management's choices of *which attractive opportunities* to pursue and which *alarming warning signals* to address. *Plans* should also describe *how* all this will be accomplished. For each choice, objectives must be set and an action plan developed describing the work to be done, by whom, to what timetable, and with what accountabilities and resources. These plans must be aligned and integrated with the business' strategic and operating plans.

There are two distinct phases in the work required to formulate these plans. The first phase is deciding which opportunities to pursue and which warning signals to address. This task requires both analytical and creative thinking. The second phase is formulating action plans describing the work involved to pursue each choice and how the organization will do this. This task is primarily creative.

The starting point for the Phase 1 work is the screened, prioritized list of attractive opportunities and alarming warning signals described in the preceding section. From this list is selected those attractive opportunities that represent the best fit with the business' strategy and cultural values. The opportunities selected should also offer the best potential returns for the resources required. The warning signals to be addressed should be those that pose the greatest risk of danger to the organization and the success of its business strategy. This work is best done initially by a small group selected for its creative imagination and diverse functional representation (as in the Stage 1 work described in the preceding section). This group's recommendations can subsequently be reviewed and validated by a larger group of managers (as in the Stage 2 work described earlier).

In Phase 2, a proposed action plan is developed describing step-by-step, the work required to pursue each selected attractive opportunity and to address each alarming warning signal. Opportunities and warning signals are assigned to one or more small groups, one for each distinct action plan. Each action planning group of 5–6 should be comprised of managers and supervisors who are most knowledgeable about what work might be required to pursue a particular attractive opportunity or dangerous threat, and how the organization might perform this work.

Typically, these groups will have a different composition from the small group described for the Phase 1 task. Action planning groups should include lower-level managers and first-line supervisors ... people close to the day-to-day detail of organizational activity. The discussion in the preceding section about an environment stimulating and supportive to creative ideas is applicable to action planning groups.

Each action planning group formulates a *proposed* action plan. Each proposal is then critiqued, reviewed, modified and validated by the same larger, more broadly representative group of managers already described. The final step in the process for formulating plans to pursue attractive opportunities and dangerous threats is an integration of the validated action plans into a single master action program that reflects priorities and specifies accountabilities and becomes part of the business' operating plan.

Organizational Focus

A fourth driver for true success is *organizational focus* on plan execution. In organizations, a plan is a necessary prerequisite to, but insufficient for ensuring actual achievement. As will be discussed in greater detail in Chapter 5, organizations are complicated entities. Once established, they have enormous inertia and are highly resistant to change. It is difficult for organizations to learn new behaviors. Organizations are highly susceptible to distraction and dysfunction.

Any plan to pursue attractive opportunities and address alarming warning signals requires an organization to do new and possibly unfamiliar things. It requires reordered priorities. The work required to execute this plan competes with all the organization's existing work. Because such a plan collides with the ongoing work of the organization, it will generate conflicts in the way resources are allocated.

This includes not only funding but also people and time. For these reasons, most plans fail in execution.

Only when an organization sustains focus over time on executing a plan will it actually achieve its objectives. This is a formidable task for the leadership. How well it succeeds in overcoming organizational inertia and managing inevitable conflict determines how close the organization can come to realizing true success. Of the four drivers for true success, organizational focus is the most critical. It is also the most difficult to achieve. How such focus can be accomplished and sustained will be described and discussed in Chapter 6.

Closing the Loop

In achieving sustained organizational focus, a key element is a systematic process for tracking and monitoring plan implementation. This enables the application of what is learned to revising and updating the plan when necessary. No one can accurately predict the future. Every plan depends on certain assumptions about future developments, but these are really based on probabilities and guesswork. A tracking and monitoring process is crucial for following up whether or not assumptions are holding, and if not, how to adjust the plan.

An effective tracking and monitoring process includes continuous reviews of operating system performance. The process should also include continuous scans of the organization's external environment. This enables detection of new developments in the industry and validation or revision of anticipated trends. Thus, both external and internal information can be kept current, ensuring a sound basis for management's ongoing understanding of what is going on both within and outside the organization ... the starting point for identifying potential new opportunities and warning signals.

Critical Organizational Capabilities

An organization's true success is driven by management's understanding of its external environment and internal situation, its identification of attractive opportunities and alarming threats, plans to address these, and organizational focus to ensure successful plan execution. In order for management to be successful in achieving these four drivers, four organizational capabilities are critical. Two are systemic: (1) a dynamic mechanism for targeting and gathering relevant external and internal information; and (2) a change-focused process for plan formulation and execution, monitoring and updating. The other two are more personal: (3)

skills in analysis, interpretation, learning and innovation; and (4) an appropriate executive mind-set.

A System for Organizational Navigation and Guidance (SONG)

By instituting and applying with rigor and discipline a formal system for organizational navigation and guidance (henceforth referred to as SONG), management gains control over the four drivers of true success. By instituting SONG, management also ensures that its organization has three of the four critical capabilities required for true success. It becomes proficient in understanding on a continuous basis, its external environment and internal situation. It identifies and addresses attractive opportunities and alarming threats. It develops skills in analysis, interpretation, learning and monitoring.

SONG thus becomes the core process for governing and managing the organization and its businesses. It enables management to set more appropriate objectives for the organization. It provides mechanisms for information targeting and gathering. It provides forums, frameworks and tools for executives and managers to work together to transform information into meaning and understanding, and to determine which opportunities are truly worth pursuing, which threats must be addressed, and how to accomplish all this. SONG also provides a framework, tools and means for ensuring effective plan execution, learning from implementation experience and the application of that learning to modifying plans to ensure that they remain current and on-target.

SONG consists of eleven or more distinct elements which must be orchestrated and synchronized into an ongoing working system and process. As management works with this system and process from year to year, it becomes increasingly skilled in its use. The full potential power of SONG to ensure true success for the organization is realized. This is described and discussed in greater detail in Chapters 6 and 7.

An Appropriate Executive Mind-Set

The fourth critical organizational capability for true success is an appropriate executive mind-set. "Appropriate" means recognition of and buy-in to the following beliefs by those in top-level leadership roles.

-   Success for an organization cannot be defined simply by fixed absolutes; rather it depends on a variety of criteria, all which can change over time.

- There is no single key to success.

- No objective or plan can be regarded as valid for more than several months; continuous changes in the organization's external environment and internal situation require periodic reviews and adjustments to both objectives and plans.

- Fundamental to an organization's ability to be truly successful is its ability on a continuing basis to identify and make appropriate changes in the way it operates.

- Changing the way an organization behaves is very difficult and requires substantial effort and time; organizations can resist change more intensely than individual people.

Only when the actions of senior executives are driven by these five beliefs will they gain full benefit and power from SONG. Otherwise, it will degenerate into empty ritual.

NOTES TO CHAPTER 3

1 By the phrase "more art than science" I mean that choices depend substantially on the exercise of judgment, tradeoffs and compromise. The issues are messy and cannot be resolved by formulas.

2 Broad, long term aspirations or statement of direction, within which shorter-term goals and objectives will fit over time. This term and concept was first introduced by G. Hamel and C. K. Prahalad in their article, Strategic Intent, *Harvard Business Review*, May-June 1989.

3 The notion of an organization's core competencies was discussed by G. Hamel and C.K. Prahalad in their articles, The Core Competence of the Corporation, *Harvard Business Review*, May-June 1990, and Corporate Imagination and Expeditionary Marketing, *The Harvard Business Review*, July-August 1991. The concept of an organization's capabilities was discussed by G. Stalk, P. Evans and L.E. Shulman in Competing on Capabilities: The New Rules of Corporate Strategy, *Harvard Business Review*, March-April 1992.

4 I have borrowed this term from T. Levitt who coined the term, marketing myopia in Chapter 8 pp141–172, *The Marketing Imagination*,

5 A leading economic theorist of the principle of "increasing returns" is W. Brian Arthur of Stanford University and the Santa Fe Institute.

6 Organizational culture is discussed by T.E. Deal and A.A. Kennedy in their book, *Corporate Cultures*, Addison-Wesley, Reading, Mass., 1982, S.M. Davis in his book, *Managing Corporate Culture*, Ballinger, Cambridge, Mass., 1984, and A.S. Judson in his book, *Changing Behavior in Organizations*, Blackwell, Oxford, U.K., 1991.

7 The concept of operating systems is discussed by A. S. Judson in his book, *Making Strategy Happen*, Blackwell, Oxford, U.K., 1996.

8 The literature dealing with innovation and creativity is extensive. Three early works are R. M. Hainer, S. Kingsbury and D. B. Gleicher's editing of a series of papers published by Reinhold, New York in 1967 under the title of *Uncertainty in Research, Management and New Product Development*, D. A. Schon's *Technology and Change*, Delacorte, New York, 1967, and W.J.J. Gordon's *Synectics*, Collier-Macmillan, New York, 1968. This last work contains an excellent analysis and discussion of creative thinking by groups. More recent works are: P. Senge, *The Fifth Discipline*; H. Takeuchi's *The Knowledge Creating Company: How Japanese Companies Create the Dynamics of Innovation*, Oxford University Press, Oxford, U.K.,1996; E. DeBono, *Serious Creativity*, Harper Business,N.Y., N.Y., 1992; D. Deacon, *Think Out Of The Box*, Career Press, Franklin Lakes, N.J., 1997; and G. Nadler & S. Hibino, *Creative Solution Finding*, Prima, Rocklin, CA, 1995.

CHAPTER 4

SETTING APPROPRIATE OBJECTIVES

Our definition of true success for organizations (Chapter 2) includes management's ability to set "appropriate" objectives on a continuing basis. The nature of organizational objectives, how they are set, and the meaning of "appropriate" are all discussed in this chapter.

Organizational Purpose and Stake Holders

Every organization exists to serve some purpose. Business organizations provide products and services to customers, and by so doing, support and enrich their stake-holders ... shareholders, suppliers, management, employees and their unions, and the communities where the firms' facilities are located. Government organizations (including the military) make, enforce and administer laws, regulations and directives that enable societies of people to function securely, peaceably, safely and to achieve a measure of well-being. Not-for-profit organizations provide at modest cost, services and products serving the interests of society in the arts, education, health and welfare, and the environment.

Like business firms, government and not-for-profit organizations have multiple stake-holders. Each government organization is concerned with the "customers" it serves, suppliers, elected officials who provide any oversight and relevant legislation and regulation, other related government agencies and departments, taxpayers, employees and their unions, management, and the communities where facilities are located. In addition to their customers, suppliers, employees, unions, management and communities, not-for-profit organizations are also concerned with a variety of funding sources and regulatory bodies, including government organizations.

Beyond their effect on stake-holders, organizations can impact society as a whole, regionally, nationally and globally. A business' product may be unsafe or have a detrimental impact on people and the environment. A university or medical center may be engaged in research with broad adverse or beneficial implications for humanity. A zoo may be able to help safeguard endangered species.

Once established, an organization defines its particular niche and long-term mission or purpose. To fulfill this, it carries out work on a continuing basis. In doing so, its leaders may see opportunities to expand and improve offerings to customers. They may also see opportunities to enhance the organization's value and benefit its stake-holders. They may need to change what the organization does or how it operates in order to deal with external changes in competition, customer wants and needs, technology, legislation and regulation, and other changes in economic, social and political matters.

The Nature of Objectives

Every objective (or goal ... I see little or no distinction) is a specified desired organizational outcome at some explicit future time. Some objectives can be quantified.

> "By the year 2012, we will increase our X business by 75%." "By the year 2010, 50% of our revenues and 67% of our profits will be generated by our Y and Z businesses." "By the year 2009, our deficit will be reduced through fund raising to less than $50,000." By the year 2011, we will reduce our operating costs to 70% of current levels."

Other objectives are more qualitative.

> "We will maintain an investment grade credit rating." "We will increase employee ownership in our Company". "We will place a man on the moon before the end of this decade." "We will expand and diversify the client populations we serve to include those who are emotionally and intellectually disabled." "We will become a leader and model in protecting and preserving our environment."

Mission or Strategic Intent

There is a three-layered hierarchy of organizational objectives. At the highest level is an organization's mission, purpose or strategic intent. Desired outcomes are stated broadly, typically in a few sentences. Described in qualitative terms are the position and role that leaders want their organization to attain several decades hence in its industry and in society as a whole.

An organization's mission statement should provide everyone impacted ... investors, funders, employees, customers, suppliers, etc., a clear statement of intended direction. Like a beacon, a mission statement serves as a steady reference point ... enabling everyone concerned to determine whether or not the organization is "on course". A good mission statement should also inspire its audience ... providing them a vision of what true success means for the organization (I see little useful distinction between statements of mission and vision). In some instances, mission statements may also include summaries of the organization's espoused values and operating principles.

Here are some examples of actual mission statements:

"We will be the preferred provider of financial products and services primarily to professional field associates and financial institutions. By providing value-added services with excellence, integrity and enthusiasm, we will enable these advisors and institutions to enhance their client's financial security, and assure our collective profitability."

"We will become a leading provider of products and services in selected markets that insure and coordinate the delivery of high-quality, cost-effective health care for individuals and employers with under 25 lives. We will primarily use X's retail distribution system to penetrate those target markets. We will support our products with best-in-class customer service and information access."

"We will be the best company in the southeast (USA) by: (a) being the preferred provider of the energy needs of our customers; (b) providing a corporate culture of mutual trust and respect, which attracts, retains and empowers a diversity of outstanding employees; (c) being widely recognized for our responsible community and environmental leadership; and (d) meeting our shareholders' expectations of long-term profitability."

"We continue to serve people primarily with mental disabilities. We are dedicated to changing perceptions: (a) of persons with disabilities about their abilities and options; (b) of employers about the capabilities of people with disabilities; and (c) of the community at large about the contributions made by people with disabilities. We seek to accomplish this by providing choices and opportunities for work for those with disabilities, and for those who experience similar barriers to employment. By providing opportunities for meaningful work and growth, we can enhance the quality of life of the individuals and communities we serve."

"We will be a North American-based, internationally recognized leader in the development, production and marketing of agricultural products ... primarily fertilizers. We will be an acknowledged benchmark in the creation of shareholder value by maintaining a strong customer focus, sustaining continual innovation, continuously improving performance and accountability, and exploiting opportunities to strengthen our competitive position."

"We are deeply committed to strengthening families, promoting healthy homes, and creating lasting connections in Greater Boston and beyond."

Strategic Business Objectives

Below the level of mission and strategic intent is the next level of organizational objectives, strategic. For each distinct "business" being conducted (see Chapter 3), there is a set of strategic objectives. Each strategic business objective generally addresses one of five subjects. The three most common are growth (typically revenue, but might also include geographic), financial performance, or improvements in operating efficiency and effectiveness. The other two topics are the nature and quality of market offerings (products and services), and desired changes in relationships with external forces (e.g. regulators, the media, funders, investors, financial analysts, the public, etc.).

These objectives' time horizon is considerably less than that of a mission ... typically 3–7 years. The focus of strategic objectives is primarily external to the organization, specifying changes that it wants to achieve for a particular business relative to markets, customers, competitors, funders and other elements of its environment. There may also be a few internally focused strategic objectives dealing with changes required to the way the organization works to enhance the achievement of external objectives. Strategic objectives are both quantitative and qualitative.

Every organization's leaders make decisions intended to take advantage of opportunities, and to make changes adapting to external developments and dealing with stake-holders' interests. These decisions spawn new objectives for the organization. Often, these require the organization to change some of its accustomed ways of operating. For example, it may need to become more innovative in its product and service offerings. It may need to take new initiatives to seek out new kinds of customers as well as improving the loyalty of existing ones. It may need to speed up the time taken to bring out new products and services. It may need to revise work processes to improve product and service quality and consistency, or reduce operating costs. It may need to establish or move to new operating locations, domestic and abroad. It may need to improve its impact on the environment. It may need to reorder priorities to achieve a better balance in serving the interests of stake-holders and society in general.

Here are some examples of statements of strategic objectives:

"Achieve and maintain quality leadership in services provided, recognized by both customers and suppliers … this will drive growth and customer retention."

"Maintain an annual growth rate so that we: (a) achieve $X million in revenues by the year Y; (b) achieve Z affiliates and W financial institutions by the year Y; and (c) position and structure ourselves to act opportunistically on attractive major acquisitions while monitoring and controlling growth so as not to sacrifice service quality and fiscal integrity."

"Decrease by 40% our dependence on box-office revenues by developing additional funding sources."

"Provide energy and related services that satisfy at least 90% of our customers (by customer class)."

"Achieve recognition as an environmental leader by our customers and regulators."

"Achieve an internal organizational environment that encourages open communication and faster decision making by reducing organizational layers, increasing spans of control. and pushing decision making down to lower levels."

"Achieve a rank within the top two (in $ revenues) in each selected targeted market within two years of entry."

"Achieve by the year X, a total product cost that is Y% below that of our top 3 competitors."

"Increase community-based and community-funded programs to a meaningful number of client served."

Consider a sequence of major changes in objectives made by the rehabilitation agency referred to in Chapter 1.

> Buoyed by increasing income from more clients provided to its largest contractor-employer, the agency's Board of Directors and Chief Executive Officer (CEO) in the early 1990s set new objectives. These aimed at growth (new employment sites) and development of new programs to attract new clients. An important underlying aim was to reduce the agency's dependence (and vulnerability) on its largest contractor, accounting at that time for almost two-thirds of the agency's total revenues.
>
> A year later, with no advance notice, that contractor cut drastically its business with the agency. The agency immediately lost about a third of its anticipated revenues. Overnight, the agency's financial position changed from accustomed modest surpluses, to rapidly increasing debt. Prior objectives were replaced by the need for dramatic cost reduction to enable survival. Concurrently, there were also changes in state and federal funding and legislative environments. The climate was no longer favorable for smaller social agencies. The Board and CEO agreed that the agency's principal objective was to find an appropriate partner and consummate a merger. If this proved unsuccessful, a fall-back position was to pare operations to the minimum financially viable scope.

Strategic Corporate Objectives

When an organization is conducting more than a single business (remember that this is as relevant for not-for-profit and government organizations as it is for profit-making businesses), the entire corporate entity has a set of strategic objectives that are distinct from those of each of its separate businesses. While these *corporate* strategic objectives have the same characteristics as strategic business objectives (i.e. time horizon, external focus, quantitative and qualitative), their nature is different. Rather than being specific to a particular business, corporate strategic objectives concern the corporate entity as a whole.

A corporate strategic objective may address any of the five subjects of strategic business objectives (growth, financial performance, operational efficiency and effectiveness, nature and quality of market offerings, and changes to external relationships), but the concern is with total corporate rather than individual business performance. An additional subject unique to corporate strategic objectives is changes in the composition of the corporate portfolio of businesses (by merger, acquisition and divestiture). Corporate objectives concerning improvements in operating effectiveness and efficiency focus on relationships and interactions *among* the corporation's various businesses and supporting functions (i.e. human resources, finance, information services, etc.), rather than what is going on within a single business or function. Here are some examples of corporate objectives.

"Maintain an overall corporate growth rate and profitability sufficient to ensure continued independence for the corporation." (e.g. a defense against any attempted takeovers)

"Develop at least X new funding sources by the year Y to support current and new services and programs within our various 'businesses' and increase Agency visibility in the community in support of our financial goals."

"By the year 2010, improve our corporate growth rate by four percentage points; achieve by acquisition and divestiture a better balance within our portfolio of fast- and slow-growth businesses."

"To become a more truly global corporation, by 2009 change the makeup of the top three management levels in our corporation so that these are staffed at least 40% by non-U.S. nationals."

"Within the next 18 months, institute a formal strategic management system and process as the principal core process for managing the corporation."

Tactical Objectives

The third level of organizational objectives is tactical. In contrast to the external orientation of strategic objectives, tactical objectives are focused primarily on changing the way things work within the organization (specifically operating systems ... see Chapter 3) in order to improve the probability of achieving strategic objectives. Tactical objectives typically address business processes in order to improve productivity, shorten process times, improve quality, reliability and predictability of both products and services and of the work environment, improve innovation, and reduce costs. Tactical objectives are typically more quantitative than qualitative, and have a short time horizon ... seldom more than two years. Here are some examples.

"Reduce by 50% time-to-market for new products (i.e. the time elapsed from initial product inception to the delivery of the first lot to customers) within the next 30 months."

"Within the next 18 months, improve customer satisfaction so that more than 95% of our customers consistently respond 'satisfied' or 'very satisfied' when surveyed."

"Within the next 24 months, reduce the cost of our services by 30% without degrading quality and customer satisfaction."

"By the end of 2008 without adding staff, double the business support services we provide to our line manager 'customers' while maintaining the high quality fiduciary reporting services we provide to our Corporate Treasurer's Office."

"Within the next 20 months, improve employee retention by 8 percentage points."

Congruency of Objectives

Within this hierarchy of objectives ... mission (corporate and business), corporate strategic, business strategic and tactical ... congruency is crucial. This means that when one views the hierarchy from top->down, the mission defines an "envelope" within which all other objectives must fit in a consistent way. Viewing the hierarchy from the bottom->up the objectives at each level must support those at the next higher level. All objectives are aligned with one another. Thus, tactical objectives support and enable the achievement of strategic business objectives; strategic business objectives support and enable the achievement of corporate strategic objectives (in the case of multi-business corporations); and all strategic objectives serve the interests of the mission.

When an organization's hierarchy of objectives is highly congruent and in alignment, the organization is positioned strongly to achieve its goals. When the hierarchy is incongruent and misaligned, the result within the organization is widespread misperception, misunderstanding and confusion. This substantially weakens the organization's ability to achieve its objectives.

Consider, for example, a global multi-business corporation headquartered in the United Kingdom. The corporation's primary strategic objective was to change the nature of its portfolio of businesses. In order to accelerate growth, corporate leaders wanted to shift a substantial portion of assets (through acquisitions) into businesses participating in industries that were faster-growing (e.g. travel and tourism) than those of the corporation's existing businesses (publishing and retailing). Corporate executives were counting on the firm's two largest businesses to provide the cash to finance their intended acquisitions. Both these businesses were no longer growing, but were cash-rich.

Neither management of these business units understood corporate's objective of changing the portfolio of businesses. Nor did they realize that corporate was expecting them to finance the acquisitions. Instead, each of their business strategies was aimed at rekindling the growth of their publishing and retail businesses. They wanted to apply their cash surpluses to acquiring other publishing and retail firms within their industries. When their strategic proposals were reviewed and rejected by corporate, they were outraged and demoralized.

How then, can all levels of an organization's management ensure that their objectives are in close alignment? This is no simple task. The larger and more complex the organization (e.g. multiple businesses and locations), the more challenging is this problem.

Setting valid objectives must take into account three factors: (1) the realities of an organization's external environment: (2) its internal capabilities: and (3) the interests of its various stake-holders. Clearly, management's understanding of all three factors must be accurate and current. Further, it must also understand any trends of change that may be occurring. Setting valid objectives depends on the quality of information gathered and its interpretation. When information is sketchy and its interpretation faulty, the quality of objectives set is degraded. The greater the organizational "distance" (number of organizational levels and extent of geographic separation) between those setting the objectives and those involved in achieving them, the greater the chances of misunderstanding and ignorance.

Considering that there is a hierarchy of objectives, it would appear that the best way to ensure alignment is to set these objectives in a linear, sequential way. Define the mission first, then set corporate strategic objectives, then strategic business objectives and finally, tactical objectives. This is possible when the organization is relatively small, carrying on only a single business out of one location. But in larger, more complex situations, top executives often are insufficiently informed about some of the businesses and external environments involved. They cannot have the understanding of those closer to the day-to-day operating realities. Corporate strategic objectives set by top executives often reflect more wishful thinking than reality. Such objectives lack credibility to those lower and more remote in the organization who must then set strategic business and tactical objectives. Once there is a question of credibility, the integrity of the entire planning and implementation process is undermined.

An alternative, more effective way to achieve a congruent set of objectives is to take an iterative approach. When top executives first define mission and set corporate strategic objectives, they do so *provisionally*. This means that they acknowledge their vulnerability to insufficient or faulty information and understandings. They make explicit that the objectives they set are no more than a first cut, subject to further revision and refinement as information and understandings improve. They invite feedback and suggestions from business unit managers as they formulate strategic business objectives.

Business unit managers, in turn, set their strategic business objectives provisionally, subject to validation and revision as operating unit managers formulate tactical objectives for their respective operating systems. No objective is "set in stone" until every manager involved in conducting a business ... top corporate executives, business unit heads, functional and operating unit managers ... have had the opportunity to examine implications and options, test the credibility of the provisional objectives, and provide feedback and comments on their conclusions.

Clearly, this approach is messy. Anyone craving neatness and tidiness will find it uncomfortable. But it works, generating a set of objectives that are aligned and internally consistent ... a key element of an effective SONG.

Making Changes

All objectives change. Strategic objectives, both corporate and business, change as organizational leaders anticipate or respond to changes in their external environments. Tactical objectives change more frequently as strategic objectives change and as changes occur within the organization itself. An organization's ability to make timely, appropriate changes in objectives relates to its ability to adapt to internal and external changes.

How well an organization does these things is crucial. "Doing these things" has three stages. First is *recognizing* opportunities, external changes and shifts in stake-holders' interests which require the organization to respond and act. Second is deciding *what actions* to take. And third is deciding *when* to act. "Well" is defined by: (1) efficient use of organizational resources, (2) speed and (3) smoothness of execution and resolution of conflict and difficulties. These arise when required changes to an organization's way of operating collide with both accustomed ways of doing things and its culture … people's values and attitudes that have developed along with their habits of behavior.

Such collisions account for most of the difficulties (noted in Chapter 1) in achieving lasting changes in the way organizations work. Prospective changes are resisted when they are seen to threaten accustomed ways of doing things, established relationships, and cherished beliefs and views. Such resistance can be individual, group, and systemic. Efforts to change the workings of organizations, however urgent and justified, are often defeated by the formidable power of this resistance.

Consider what happened when the CEO set increased sales and profit objectives for North America's leading paint manufacturer. He wanted to turn around a slow but steady erosion of this century-old firm's leading share of a highly fragmented market. The company had been losing market share because consumers were no longer willing to pay premium prices for its high quality paint. Its many competitors had improved the quality of their paint to the point where customers were unable to detect the leader's supposed superior quality. These facts were confirmed both by independent testing organizations and by several market studies commissioned by the company.

The organization's response to the CEO's new objectives was ineffectual. The firm's advertising budget was increased. Promotional and sales efforts were intensified. More resources were applied to ongoing programs aimed at increasing productivity in the company's many plants. Yet these were operating at greatly reduced capacity because of eroding sales. Continued sales decline canceled any gains from productivity improvement. The company's performance continued to sag.

The organization resisted making any basic change in its existing strategy, trading on its reputation for high quality paint, and focusing on operating efficiencies. In a market where paint was now seen as a commodity with price the customer's prime concern, only a new strategy of aggressive pricing could have enabled the company to regain lost market share. But price cuts were unthinkable. In the firm's culture, a cherished belief was the highest quality paint deserved a premium price. So strong was this belief that when faced with new objectives, management and employees simply continued to do more intensely what they had been doing all along. They discounted market studies confirming that consumers saw paint as a commodity.

Management is responsible and accountable for the decisions and actions needed to recognize opportunities and external changes, and for determining whether, how and when its organization should respond. Management must set objectives for the organization, decide on a course of action (or strategy) to achieve these objectives, and manage the execution of whatever changes must be made to implement the strategy. All these areas of management decision-making are discussed in this book: the first below, and the others in Chapters 6 and 7.

Setting Appropriate Objectives

So far in this chapter, I have discussed the nature and types of objectives relevant to any organization. Now consider what is involved when a particular executive, manager, or management group sets a specific objective, strategic or tactical.

Factors That Influence Objective Setting

When setting objectives, an organization's leaders consider several different factors. One is the nature and attractiveness of opportunities in the organization's external environment. For a business, this means the kind and intensity of customers' unsatisfied needs or unsolved problems, along with the nature and strength of competitors' products and services. For a not-for-profit educational institution, this may mean people's needs for particular kinds of knowledge and skills unmet by existing educational programs. For a museum it may mean exhibits on little-known subjects or by younger, up-and-coming artists. For a government agency, it may mean offering ancillary services such as information and education to enhance compliance with regulations and electronic filing for taxpayers.

Another factor influencing objective setting is constraints limiting the organization's ability to act. Such constraints can be internal such as a shortage of resources (funds, time, skills and competencies), or weaknesses in organizational capability (effective new product development, flexibility in how work gets processed). Constraints can also be external (lack of distribution capability, legislation and regulation, lack of critical sources of supply, unavailability of capital or other sources of funding).

A third factor that may influence objectives is existing strong organizational capabilities which can be leveraged. For example, leaders of an organization with a strong cash position may pursue growth or diversification through acquisitions. If there is a strong research and development capability, management's objectives may depend on product innovation. If the organization has strong operational capabilities with unused capacity, management may pursue growth seeking new customers in new areas.

Yet another factor influencing objectives are the interests and demands of the organization's various stake-holders. These include key customers and suppliers, shareholders, investment analysts, major funders (for not-for-profit and government organizations), political pressure groups (for government organizations), the organization's own employees and unions, and members of communities where the organization is located. For example, a business with substantial surplus cash must set ambitious growth objectives often involving acquisitions in order both to be perceived by the investment community as deploying its assets productively and to defend itself from being acquired. A social agency may embark on new programs in order to appeal to funding sources with special interests.

There is also an ethical factor in setting objectives. Every organization must operate within the law, not only its letter but also its spirit. When times are good or bad, any benefits or cutbacks should be shared fairly among stake-holders. For example, a business' employees as well as its executives and shareholders should benefit in periods of profitability. When competitive pressures lead to downsizing and restructuring, a firm's leadership and shareholders should not and should not be seen as benefiting at the expense of employees whose jobs are vanishing. Consideration for consequences on society must influence every objective. Whenever there are opportunities to contribute to the creation of a more humane society, the leadership of every organization should recognize these and act accordingly.

> Recently, many U.S. businesses have been focusing on increasing shareholder value at the expense of other considerations. In a study of some 400 large corporations reported in *Business Week*, average shareholder value increased 76% from 1990–95. In the same period, average CEOs' compensation rose 97%, but average employees' wages improved only 16%. This behavior in a climate of extensive corporate downsizing gave rise in 1996 to sharp criticism both by public officials and in the media. A few CEOs in Massachusetts who acted more ethically were singled out as notable exceptions and publicly praised. The President of Malden Mills continued to pay his workers during a shutdown caused by a devastating fire. To share unusually high profits, the CEO of Citizens Bank unexpectedly distributed a sizable midyear bonus to all employees. Although such acts would have received little attention in earlier years, they were publicized widely in 1996 as exceptional.

In mid-June 1997, *The Boston Globe* reported that Harvard University had for six years been surreptitiously (through a "straw", the Beals Cos.) buying up 52 acres of real estate in Allston, a Boston neighborhood adjacent to the Harvard Business School and Harvard's athletic fields (the rest of Harvard's real estate is in Cambridge, across the Charles River from Boston) (1). When confronted with its actions, Harvard officials acknowledged a "breach of trust" but claimed that the university had no specific plans for the Allston property. Efforts by Boston's Mayor Thomas M. Menino to extract "reparations" (in the form of additional scholarships for Boston residents) from Harvard in exchange for allowing it to proceed with its development plans in Allston were rebuffed. Several years later, Harvard revealed detailed plans for an extensive new Boston campus on the Allston property. Here is a prime example of failure to consider ethical issues in setting objectives.

A fifth and often controlling factor determining objectives is the personal agendas of key executives. The ambitions and vision of the top leader is often crucial. An important issue is tradeoffs that senior managers are willing to make between ambitious achievements, widespread public recognition and financial gain on the one hand, and hard work, long hours and total commitment to the enterprise on the other.

Weighting the Factors and Leaders' Agendas

When objectives are set, the relative importance assigned to each of these factors depends on leaders' personalities and the organization's circumstances.

An engineer I knew founded a company in his garage to produce and market a line of temperature control devices based on his invention. His initial objective was simply to earn enough to finance his wife's doctoral degree. Although he was not aggressive in encouraging sales, the company's growth exceeded his wildest expectations. As the product's superior technical capabilities gained widespread acceptance, the firm grew to employ more than 600. Early on, he set another qualitative objective for the organization and its employees. Impressed with the teachings of Douglas McGregor, he wanted his organization to operate on "Theory Y" management principles, where employees were treated with respect and could satisfy their needs for self-actualization.

In another example, Edwin Land perceived in 1948 an unmet customer need (without benefit of market research) for "instant" photographic prints. To address the opportunity he invented a self-developing photographic system. Polaroid Corporation (to this point a moderately successful producer of specialty optical products) became one of America's first high-flying hi-tech companies in the 1950s and 60s. Land's personal agenda and interests determined Polaroid's objectives. He wanted continued financial and technical resources to support his passion for research and invention. He wanted to create an innovative organization where employees would find work "fun" and have opportunities to develop their talents and capabilities. He also wanted to maintain his control over the organization despite the fact that Polaroid was a publicly owned corporation with Land holding less that 12% of its shares.

In not-for-profit and government organizations, leaders' personal agendas play no less important a part in objective setting. However, personal gain is typically defined less in financial terms and more in terms of public service, acclaim and personal power.

Appropriate Objectives

In assessing whether or not an organization can be deemed successful, the nature of its objectives is but one critical consideration. The other is how effectively and consistently they are actually achieved. Assessment of objectives should be made in terms of their *appropriateness*.

An objective is *appropriate* when it stems from an explicit, systematic consideration of: (1) external opportunities; (2) limiting constraints; (3) organizational capabilities; (4) stake-holders' and societal interests; and (5) personal agendas. Objectives should not be set arbitrarily or "pulled out of the air" by the organization's chief. Rather, they should reflect consensus among the organization's senior executives after they carefully consider and weight each factor. Special attention should be given to the consequences of each objective on stake-holders and its impact on society as a whole.

Appropriateness also has to do with the ambitiousness of each objective … how much of a stretch is required by the organization to reach it. The trick here is to set goals that are demanding but not unreasonable. From schoolchildren in classrooms to giant corporations there is considerable evidence that expectations influence performance. When expectations are high and demanding, performance tends to be better than when expectations are low. Incremental goals tend to result in incremental improvements. Stretch goals often yield giant gains.

Two cautionary notes should be sounded. Credible rationales are needed to support stretch goals. Pressure arising from competitors' performance can provide convincing evidence. Similarly, studies of best operating practices both within and outside an industry where processes are comparable, can also justify and enhance credibility. The other note of caution is not to expect people to respond to stretch goals simply by working harder and longer hours. This only raises stress levels and demoralizes the very people who must deliver the goods. When stretch goals are set, needed additional resources must be provided. This includes skills, tools, funding, and staff.

In the early 1990s, the CEO of 3M (Minnesota Mining & Manufacturing), a company admired for its product innovation, set a stretch goal to accelerate this activity. 3M's traditional product innovation target had been to generate 25% of its sales from new products introduced in the prior five years. The new stretch goal was to generate 30% of revenues from new products introduced in the prior four years. The CEO of Mead, a large U.S. paper manufacturer, set in 1991 a stretch goal of increasing annual productivity improvement tenfold by the end of the decade. In 1992, the CEO of Boeing decided that it was crucial for the aircraft manufacturer to make it cheaper for airlines to buy new planes than to repair and operate old ones. He set a stretch goal of reducing the cost of aircraft manufacture 25% by 1998. By mid-1995, all three of these firms had already made dramatic progress towards meeting these ambitious objectives.

NOTES TO CHAPTER 4

1 *The Boston Globe*, Vol. 251 Nos. 162 & 163, 11 and 12 June 1997

CHAPTER 5

WHY ORGANIZATIONAL NAVIGATION AND GUIDANCE IS SO CRITICAL

At the end of Chapter 3, I suggest that a system for organizational navigation and guidance (SONG)) is the best, most powerful means for a management to gain leverage on the forces that drive its organization's success. Also, in each of the foregoing chapters, there are allusions with examples to organizations' complexity and how difficult it is to achieve changes in the way they operate. How is it, then, that SONG has such power and is so effective? In this chapter I discuss more fully the nature of organizations, how and why they resist change, and what it takes to achieve durable changes in the way they operate.

The Nature of Organizations

Any organization of more than a few people is an extraordinarily unwieldy entity. Once established, every organization takes on a life of its own. Its accustomed ways of behaving become highly resistant to any attempted changes. My favorite definition is that an organization is an unnatural act performed by consenting adults in public. Why do I take such a dim view?

Organizations As Systems

Every organization is a complex system comprised of nine major elements.

1. People (individual competencies, capabilities, interests, aspirations and potential)

2. Structure
- ➤ organizational levels (hierarchy) and reporting relationships
- ➤ job design, responsibilities and accountabilities

➤ definitions of businesses, business units, operating units and supporting functions

3. Business processes

4. Formal supporting systems
➤ controls, measures and monitoring
➤ information
➤ budgeting
➤ planning
➤ communications
➤ rewards and compensation

5. Formal policies and procedures

6. Mission and objectives, strategic and tactical

7. Priorities

8. Technology: process, product, equipment, facilities

9. Culture (beliefs, values and behavioral norms)

As an organization performs work to fulfill its purpose (see Chapter 4), these nine elements interact continuously and dynamically, each with all the other eight. While this is going on, the system as a whole is impacted continuously by six external forces.

I. Customers, their expectations, needs and wants

II. Industry, market, funder, and competitor dynamics and trends

III. Associations and affiliation groups (industry/trade associations, trade unions, professional associations)

IV. Governmental regulations (federal, state, local)

V. Technological developments and trends

VI. Social, economic and political developments and trends

These external forces along with changes to any system element, cause changes at varying magnitudes and rates of frequency to each of the other elements of the system. People leave and are replaced. New people are added. People are trained. Organization and job structures are redesigned. Businesses, business and operating units and functions are redefined. Business processes and formal supporting systems are redesigned. Policies and procedures are rewritten. Objectives are changed and priorities reordered. Technology keeps changing.

As with all systems, any change to one element reverberates throughout the system, affecting other elements. Often, a deliberate change to one system element produces unanticipated and unintended consequences both to other elements and to the system as a whole. Only culture is slow to change.

Formal and Informal Organizations

Every organization has both a formal and informal aspect. These two aspects co-exist (often uneasily) in the same time and space. Forces influencing the behavior of the people involved (who are the same for both aspects) are typically quite different.

The formal organization is a manifestation of what is intended and espoused in official documents. People are encouraged to behave as they are *supposed to*, following formal reporting procedures, doing what is in their job descriptions, pursuing objectives as documented in formal plans, and observing recommended priorities and official systems, processes and policies and procedures. Things are supposed to be done "by the book."

In the informal organization, however, people are influenced to behave very differently. They are driven not "by the book" but rather by habit, cultural norms, beliefs and values and by established personal relationships. The grapevine and past practice takes precedence over official communiqués. Another major influence is concern for the reactions of work mates, the union or other relevant associations.

How an organization actually behaves depends on the extent to which the formal and informal organizations are "in synch." The more they are congruent, the more efficient and effective the organization performs as it sets and achieves appropriate objectives. When they are incongruent, there is a substantial gap between what is espoused and what actually happens. The result is confusion, lack of focus, broken promises, conflict, missed deadlines and waste.

Consider the experience of a British-based pharmaceutical company operating in 25 countries throughout the globe. This organization was one of three companies, each conducting a different business, but all part of a single multi-business corporation or "Group". A new Group Chairman took command when the corporation was foundering, and was successful in revitalizing all three businesses. Once "The City" (the U.K. equivalent of Wall Street) acknowledged the turnaround, the Group's share price began to climb. The Group's attractiveness as a potential takeover target increased.

As a defense against potential acquirers, the Chairman determined that a consistent track record of dramatic profit growth for the Group was necessary. Accordingly, he set a corporate strategic objective of 20% profit improvement annually. The leadership of each of the three companies assumed that they must deliver 20% profit growth to the Group each year.

The pharmaceutical company had an established strategic planning process. Every autumn, a detailed questionnaire was sent to the managements of each of the 25 country "companies". They had to answer questions about the characteristics of their local markets, customers, competitors, government regulation and other key industry developments and trends. They also had to submit a five-year plan for marketing, sales, product requirements (all research and development and most production were done centrally in the U.K.), and local production, accompanied by projected revenue and expense numbers. In February of the following year, proposed plans and numbers were aggregated and analyzed at U.K. headquarters, along with the plans from central R&D and manufacturing. Any required modifications were then made, reviewed and approved by Group management and communicated to the operating units and support functions. Their modified plans were completed by late spring, and were subsequently implemented. Every year, executives and managers throughout the company expended substantial time and effort on this process.

This planning system was meant to be the core process for managing the company. It provided the means for collecting and documenting performance promises from managers worldwide, and then holding them accountable for results. Outside observers were impressed with this process as a model organizational navigation and guidance system.

Reality within the organization was entirely different. Executives and managers, both in the U.K. and in remote locations regarded the planning process as a farce. They saw the entire system as an annual ritual, in which they were forced to participate only to satisfy headquarters. To them, neither the plans nor the accompanying numbers had any integrity or credibility. Once completed, plans were filed away for reference only at the start of next year's cycle. No one paid any attention to the plans in day-to-day operations.

Why was there such a difference between the formal and informal organizations, especially when the unutilized planning system represented squandered resources? The guidance and control system failed to perform its intended function because it was corrupted by everyone's perception that they must deliver 20% annual profit growth to the Group. In effect, the entire planning process was driven by the need to meet this numerical corporate objective.

What actually happened was the following. Each February top pharmaceutical company executives found that the aggregated promises in the proposed plans from the 25 country "companies" did not add up to the required 20% profit improvement. To make up for the shortfall, headquarters management arbitrarily and unilaterally made a number of unwarranted assumptions and decisions. They assumed that potential new products in the research and development "pipeline" would be available sooner than scheduled. They postponed funding projects specified as required in the proposed plans of both country "companies" and central R&D and manufacturing. These assumptions and decisions were not discussed with the affected parties. They were simply announced. Yet no changes were permitted in the performance promises made by the country "companies" and central functions.

Beyond the widespread lack of credibility of the entire planning system and the resultant cynicism of most senior and middle-level managers, the consequences for the company ultimately proved disastrous. But in the short term, top management's practice of mortgaging the future succeeded. For several years, the pharmaceutical company succeeded in delivering an annual profit improvement of at least 20% to the Group. Share prices climbed steadily. But the chickens eventually came home to roost. In the U.S.A. (the company's largest market), an investigation by the Food and Drug Administration uncovered quality problems with one of the firm's leading products. After this was withdrawn from the market, the source of the problem was traced to central manufacturing in the U.K., where additional quality problems were uncovered. The resultant drop in revenues and profits caused much unfavorable publicity and havoc with the share price. Soon after, the pharmaceutical company CEO resigned and the Group Chairman "retired for reasons of health".

System Performance, Size and Complexity

Every organization of more than a handful of people contains the nine elements and is subject to the six forces described earlier in the Chapter. How effectively it performs depends primarily on how well its management deals with all this. But the challenge to management escalates dramatically as the organization's size and complexity increases.

There are several ways in which size and complexity can increase. One is simply number of employees. Another is the number of departments or functions in the organization. Another is the number of different geographical locations for the organization's physical facilities (offices, warehouses, production factories, retail outlets). These locations can be concentrated within a metropolitan area, or dispersed throughout a state, province, country or the entire globe or segments thereof. Yet another way in which organizational complexity can increase is the number of discrete businesses being conducted, and the extent to which these businesses are related or different.

These different dimensions to increased size and complexity are interrelated and interdependent. All are driven by growth of the organization's business or businesses. As customers demand more of the organization's products and services, more employees are added. A function performed initially by a single individual grows into a group which then becomes a separate department. New functions and departments may be established in response to regulatory requirements (i.e. environmental, regulatory conformance, health and safety, etc.). New facilities are established to respond to demand and to service new markets. New businesses may develop either through internal innovation or through external acquisition.

Along with growth in numbers of employees, functions, locations and businesses, there is accompanying growth in organizational hierarchy. Additional levels of management and supervision are needed to oversee and coordinate the proliferation of functions, departments, locations and businesses.

All this increase in organizational size and complexity has a profound effect on the vulnerability of the organization to dysfunction and poor performance. The increased challenge to management is exponential. This is because there is a consequence common to all these different ways in which size and complexity can increase. That consequence is an increased *distance* between those making decisions and giving direction, and those who must execute in response.

Distance is physical, hierarchical and psychological. Physical distance is horizontal. Increases in physical distance can be a change from everyone working on a single floor within sight and earshot of one another, to dispersal to multiple floors in the same building, or to several locations within a radius of a few miles, or to more distant places. As physical distance increases, working/operating units become increasingly remote from key decision makers. Communications among senior executives in a headquarters office and these outlying operating units become more formal, impersonal, reliant on the written word, and top->down. Useful feedback and face-to-face interaction is increasingly difficult to achieve.

Hierarchical distance is measured in the number of organizational levels that separate the worker from the decision maker. Hierarchical distance is vertical. As organizations grow in size and complexity, the number of levels in the management hierarchy increases. Even in single-business organizations of several hundred employees operating out of one facility, there can be 4–6 layers of management and supervision between the top leader and those doing operational tasks. In giant, multi-business organizations, there can be as many as 9–10 layers. Every layer represents a link in the chain-of-command and communications. Each layer must receive and transmit *accurately* directives, suggestions, ideas, proposals and responses, both top->down and bottom->up. Each layer can introduce distortions, omissions and misinformation. The more layers, the greater the opportunities for corrupting intent.

Psychological distance stems from both physical and hierarchical distance. It shows up as gaps in understanding and thinking between those setting objectives and those responsible for achieving them. When the two are both physically and hierarchically remote from one another, opportunities for misunderstandings are rife. At operating levels, local perceptions, agendas, concerns and priorities develop and influence actual behavior more than do communications and directives from headquarters. Even when the quantity and quality of communications are excellent, they are no match for these local influences.

Organizations perform well when they consistently set and achieve appropriate objectives over time. This requires a unity of purpose, understanding and commitment by everyone throughout the organization. This is possible when an organization consists of a few people working together daily in close proximity. Objectives and supporting rationales are readily understood and enthusiastically pursued. Collaboration is easy. Differences are detected early and resolved. Progress and accomplishment is readily apparent. Motivation and esprit are high.

Yet every increase in size and complexity raises new obstacles to the above. Executives and managers must devote more and more time to communicating, listening and resolving conflicts and misunderstandings. Their best efforts cannot prevent deterioration in alignment between the formal and informal organizations. Organizational performance suffers.

Organizational Culture: A Critical Issue

Earlier, I listed culture as one of the nine elements comprising every organizational system. Culture has a strong, pervasive influence on total system behavior. Further, unlike the other eight system elements, it is slow to change. Accordingly, culture is a critical issue for understanding organizational systems and how they can be changed.

Every organization consists of one or more small societies, each with a history and culture. This is the collection of beliefs and norms of behavior that influence the daily choices and decisions that people make. Usually, these beliefs and norms are unspoken, operating below the level of consciousness. Yet their power to influence is great. They represent the residue of the organization's history ... its past leaders, accomplishments and failures and how people have come to explain them.

Here are some examples that I encountered of organizational cultural beliefs and norms. Each of these had a profound impact on the organization's performance: sometimes positive, often negative.

- If it's good for my department it's good for the entire organization.
- We care about our people.
- Most inputs from marketing are of dubious value.
- Solving immediate problems is what's really important; the longer term future will take care of itself.
- Business strategy is product strategy.
- Common goals and unified leadership for related functions and departments is not that essential for business success; internal competition is healthy.
- To maintain a nice work environment with comfortable relationships, we must be careful to avoid tough interpersonal confrontations and not be too demanding of our employees.
- The way to control costs is to watch every penny.
- It's results that count ... not how they are achieved.
- We can and should get premium prices for our products because of our name, reputation and quality.
- Sound decisions depend on having precise numbers.

Because culture results from an organization's history, larger organizations can have more than one set of norms and beliefs. This occurs when there are multiple facilities. As each facility is a physical entity with its own unique history, the norms and beliefs of the people in a particular office, factory, warehouse, retail outlet, laboratory, medical facility, etc. may be different from those in other organizational locations, even when some norms and beliefs are shared throughout the organization. This situation often becomes apparent after acquisitions and mergers. As the acquired organization has a history different from that of the acquirer, its culture is also different. Cultures that are incongruent or in conflict require lots of effort and time to meld. The high failure rate of mergers and acquisitions (66–75% (1)) can be attributed primarily to this problem.

> In the late 1990s, two adjacent hospitals in Boston, Massachusetts decided to merge ... the Beth Israel and New England Deaconess. Both hospitals were long-standing, well established institutions with excellent reputations. Their cultures, however, differed in some important respects. After the merger, morale dropped precipitously. There was an exodus of several leading physicians with world-class reputations. The new organization's financial performance dropped dramatically into deficits. Only after a new CEO was appointed (a non-medical person from outside the organization with a superb managerial track record) did the problems subside. It took more than five years after the merger for the new, strong leadership to restore excellent health care and financial performance.

Culture influences a wide range of management's choices and decisions. For example, culture influences management's assumptions and expectations about what people want out of work, and what they are capable of contributing. Culture influences how management defines the business(es) it is conducting along with business and functional missions. Culture affects where (hierarchical level) particular decisions are made in the organization as well as how many levels are desirable or appropriate and what should be appropriate spans of control. What is truly important (priorities) is influenced by culture. The importance of training and the resources allocated to it are partly determined by culture. Culture influences how management views communications: how much should be invested in it, and how it should flow (e.g. top->down, bottom->up, lateral). Culture affects management's thinking about how flexible or specialized people should be with regard to knowledge and skills.

Culture also affects management's thinking about sources of innovation in the organization: where (or if) one should seek suggestions for improvement, and what mechanisms are desirable to stimulate and implement new ideas. How important is planning and how much should be invested in it is influenced by culture. Likewise, culture affects management's views about control ... what needs to be controlled, to what extent and how.

Culture also determines how management views rewards, compensation and recognition. How should compensation and other forms of reward and recognition relate to performance, knowledge and loyalty/length of service? How great should be pay differentials between superior and average performers? Should there be an incentive component to compensation, and if so, to what extent? Which employees should share in company profitability, and to what extent?

Clearly, the power of culture to influence almost every aspect of how organizations work cannot be overestimated.

Organizational Inertia and Resistance to Change

Culture pervades almost every aspect of management's thinking, choices and decision-making. Values, beliefs and norms operate below the level of people's consciousness. Hence they are taken as "givens" and are seldom questioned and examined. Thus, culture is a major factor in organizational inertia.

All systems, once established, crave equilibrium. This means that all elements, as they interact with one another, move towards mutual accommodation. Once this state is reached, the system settles into a comfortable *status quo*. It has inertia. It doesn't want to change. Organizations are no exception to this scenario.

Consider the elements in any organizational system that contribute to its inertia and resistance to change. A major factor is the organizational structure and resultant established relationships among people and functions. Another factor is established work habits, rules and procedures. Another is existing work processes and supporting systems such as information, control, rewards, budgets, etc. Underlying all these factors is the organization's culture, manifested in its traditions, values, beliefs and norms. All these combine to point people towards *"customary"* behavior. "This is how we do things here." This outlook is the cement that gives great strength to organizational inertia.

The power of organizations' inertia is so great that they are more resistant to changes than are the people who inhabit them. Although individuals can be resistant to changes, personal circumstances and motivation vary widely. Individuals can be persuaded, involved and even coerced (2). But people are only one element in organizational systems. The other eight elements in concert constitute an interlocking barrier to change that is formidable (3).

What It Takes To Change the Behavior of Organizational Systems

For any organization to be truly successful, it must continuously achieve durable changes in the way it behaves internally. This means finding ways to neutralize or overcome the inertia and resistance of the organizational system. What does it take to do this when the power of inertia and resistance is so strong?

Earlier in this chapter I describe the nine elements that interact continuously in every organizational system. In order for the behavior of the system as a whole to change, *some aspect of several of these elements must change in a concerted, coordinated way.* Addressing only a single element in hopes of changing total system behavior won't work. This is because leverage on the entire system is insufficient. This is the flaw common to most of the failed panaceas noted in Chapter I that were offered in the past as keys to success.

Management Actions

To gain the power required to overcome organizational inertia and resistance, management must first identify that *combination* of elements which will provide sufficient leverage to achieve desired changes in overall system behavior. I call these elements high leverage target opportunities (4). A high leverage target opportunity is typically an organizational system element which is blocking or undermining the achievement of desired objectives. By changing this element (or an aspect thereof), the impact on changing total system behavior is disproportionately powerful to the resources applied. This concept and approach is discussed more extensively in Operating Plans, Chapter 6, Section 6.

Once management identifies the several high leverage target opportunities to address, it must reorder organizational priorities so that the organization can sustain its focus on making the desired changes. Then, management must ensure that there is an *explicit operating plan formulated for changing the organizational system.* This plan should include clear tactical objectives and priorities, a work plan detailing tasks, timetables and accountabilities, and a plan for measuring and monitoring execution.

Another requirement for changing how organizational systems work, is sustained, relentless and disciplined follow-up by every level of management to ensure that the operating plan is successfully executed. This includes making explicit the learning that occurs from the experience of implementing the plan, and applying insights gained to modifying the plan as appropriate. This ensures that the plan remains on course, on time and on target, despite unforeseen developments during implementation.

All the above management actions must be accompanied by continuous extensive communication to everyone involved. At the outset, people must be informed about the effort to change the behavior of the organizational system. This includes intended objectives, the rationale for these, how the changes will be achieved and measured, when, by whom and with what resources. The operating plan should be widely shared. As implementation proceeds, people must be kept informed about accomplishments and progress along with any changes to the plan.

Key Outcomes For Changing System Behavior

All the above management actions should be directed towards achieving five key outcomes. These are the critical factors for accomplishing successful changes in the way organizational systems work.

First, there must be a widely shared *understanding* by everyone involved of what the change effort is all about and why. People need to know what the changes are intended to achieve and how these will be accomplished and measured. Each person directly affected needs to know how, and what this will mean personally. Once the plan is being executed, people need to understand how implementation is proceeding and about any concrete accomplishments.

Second, everyone directly involved in making the changes must have *commitment* to the success of the operating plan. This is an emotion or feeling that goes beyond mere understanding. People need to *believe* that the changes are necessary, and that the plan for making the changes is *credible*. If possible, they should have a feeling of ownership in the plan and its intended outcomes.

Third, *resources* necessary for successfully executing the operating plan must be made explicit and available when needed. These include not only money, but also tools, training, time, expertise and skills.

Another critical success factor is a formal, disciplined *system and process* applied with rigor, that enables management and everyone else involved to *measure and monitor progress* in executing the operating plan. This process must include regular and systematic progress reviews by all accountable people *together*, so that they can make explicit any learning from accomplishments, unexpected problems encountered, etc., and make any needed modifications to the plan so that it remains current.

Fifth, there must be a clearly perceived *climate of accountability* so that everyone in the organization believes that commitments and promises will be taken seriously, and that there will be consequences when these are met or not met. This also presumes that accountabilities are clearly assigned and widely understood. A crucial factor here is leadership behavior where words and actions are congruent.

When a management by its actions has achieved these five outcomes, it will be able successfully to make whatever changes in its organization's behavior are needed to achieve the objectives it sets. When it establishes SONG and uses it continuously as its core process for managing its business(es) and organization, its chances for success will be greatly enhanced.

NOTES TO CHAPTER 5

1 These failure rates are based on both my personal experience and several independent studies.

2 The dynamics of individual and small group resistance to changes are discussed at length in A. S. Judson, *Changing Behavior in Organizations*, Blackwell, Oxford, U.K., 1991.

3 A particularly useful book about organizations and how they behave is C. Handy, Understanding Organizations, Oxford U. Press, N.Y., N.Y., 1993.

4 High leverage target opportunities and how to identify these are discussed at length in A.S. Judson, *Making Strategy Happen*, Blackwell, Oxford U.K., 1996

CHAPTER 6

ELEMENTS OF A SYSTEM FOR ORGANIZATIONAL NAVIGATION AND GUIDANCE (SONG)

To establish a system for organizational navigation and guidance (SONG), the management of any organization conducting a single business must institute and work with eleven distinct elements. This also applies to small organizations conducting more than one business. Each of these elements is discussed in this chapter. In Chapter 7, I describe how these eleven elements work together in an effective SONG. In large organizations conducting more than a single business, SONG requires seven additional elements for a total of eighteen. These and how they work in concert are discussed in Chapter 9.

None of SONG's eleven elements is unfamiliar. Many organizations already work with some of them. But few organizations use all eleven, and even fewer apply them in an integrated way. Furthermore, although the nomenclature for each element may appear familiar. the particular characteristics of each element required for an effective SONG may differ significantly from those typical of most organizations' experience.

1. Business Definition

An explicit definition of the organization's business is one element of SONG. Business definitions are important because they serve several different purposes. How a business is defined determines the scope and focus of the industry to be analyzed (Chapter 3). Business definitions provide frameworks for formulating business strategies ... which opportunities should be pursued and which threats must be disarmed, and how. A clear statement of "the business we are in" helps everyone in the organization understand the context for their work, so that they can relate their day-to-day tasks to "the big picture". An understanding of the

71

business definition also helps to clarify what is truly important so that the organization can achieve and sustain focus (one of the four drivers for true success noted in Chapter 3).

A business definition should reflect both the realities of the markets being addressed and the organization's internal capabilities (Chapter 3). Business definitions must be reviewed periodically to ensure that they are current with changes in the organization's external environment and internal circumstances (note examples from computer industry in Chapter 2).

No business definition should be taken for granted before formulating a strategic plan. Rather, it should be positioned as provisional, subject to validation by the planning process. This is because insights developed as this process unfolds often stimulate reformulation of the provisional definition (recall the examples in Chapter 3 of the U.K. beer company and the U.S. regional insurance company). This illustrates the need to treat the strategy formulation process as iterative, not linear. Other examples appear in the following pages.

2. Definitions of Business and Operating Units

Another element of SONG is defining those segments of the organization that are strategic business units or SBUs, and those that are operating units (OUs). This is crucial because it establishes clarity of organizational roles. SBU managers formulate and execute strategic business plans. OU managers formulate and execute operating plans. When these roles are confused, the organization's ability to achieve true success is seriously undermined (see following examples).

Once management defines the SBUs and OUs in an organization, it has established a framework for SONG. It has determined the number and scope of strategic and operating plans that must be formulated, executed and monitored.

Defining SBUs

Consider the experience of a giant global energy company. After investing several millions of dollars with help from one of the world's leading management consulting firms, a high-level corporate strategy was formulated along with a comprehensive SONG to ensure its successful execution. All this was documented in a 4.5 pound *Strategic Management System Reference Manual* for use by several thousand executives and managers throughout the company. Unfortunately, this approach, while admirable in many ways, failed to address a fundamental issue ... defining the SBUs and OUs which were expected to translate the corporate strategy into more concrete business strategies. This task was assigned to existing organizational units, structured by function and geography, not by business.

For example, an organizational unit charged with oil and gas exploration and production in Canada was defined by and located in a particular geographic/geologic area. This unit was designated an SBU and expected to formulate its own strategic business plan. This expectation proved highly frustrating (and ultimately unworkable) to the unit's managers. They were not, in fact, conducting a discrete autonomous business for which they could be held accountable. In reality they were managing an OU that supported, (along with many other similar OUs) two different businesses: North American Oil and North American Gas. No one in the company was identified as responsible and accountable for each of these businesses, and no strategic plans were formulated for them. The consequences of these improperly defined SBUs and OUs was widespread confusion, mismanaged businesses (missed opportunities and wasted resources) and a failed SONG.

There is a key distinction between SBUs and OUs. Only the former interacts and deals with markets, distributors, customers, funders and competitors *outside the organization*. The criteria and clues for defining distinct businesses are discussed early in Chapter 3. As with business definitions, definitions of SBUs and OUs must be reviewed (and modified) periodically to ensure that they remain relevant in light of changes in the organization's external environment and internal situation. Also, revisions in these definitions may occur as the strategy development process unfolds and new insights are gained.

In the late 1960s when the U.S. General Electric Company (GE) first began strategic planning, it did so after establishing organizational divisions based on product lines. Each division was designated an SBU responsible for formulating and executing its own strategy. Thus there was a refrigerator strategy, a dishwasher strategy, a washer and dryer strategy and so on. Each was developed independently of the others. Defining each division as an SBU proved to be a serious error. The parochial strategic perspective taken by each product line organization slowed GE's recognition and consideration of several important characteristics of the marketplace.

Customers expected that the kitchen and laundry appliances they purchased be coordinated in quality (materials, performance, warranties, etc.) and appearance (color, design, features, etc.). They expected coordinated pricing that unified the appliances within the context of the manufacturer's "quality and style" philosophy. Each GE division soon discovered that its competitors and distributors were similar to those faced by its sister divisions. Despite extensive overlap, each division was waging its own battle with the same set of competitors. At the corporate level, GE executives began questioning the impact of selling or dropping individual product lines on the remaining businesses. All these considerations led GE to realize (after several years of disappointing performance) that the product line-based divisions were in fact segments of a single SBU, subsequently named "white goods", for which a single strategic business plan would suffice.

A Business Need Not Be An SBU

When an organization is conducting more than a single business, these need not be treated as distinct SBUs. Businesses and SBUs are two different things. A business is a concept. An SBU is an organizational construct.

Recall the social agency described in Chapters 1, 3 and 4. Although its organization was modest in size (fewer than 50 staff), it was conducting four different businesses. One business was an in-house workshop providing contracted custom packaging services to local manufacturers. Another was staffing and supervising certain operations (e.g. packaging, assembly, etc.) for local firms on their premises. A third business with a variety of organizations was filling and supporting individual entry-level positions with the agency's clients. The agency's fourth business was finding tenants and subletting space in a large building which the agency was leasing.

Each of these businesses had its own distinct set of customers, agency clients, funders, competitors and revenue and cost characteristics. Yet none was of a scale sufficient to justify a separate organization or distinct strategic and operating plans. The agency's management recognized that it was conducting four businesses. They accounted for them and tracked their performance separately, but planned and managed them as an integrated portfolio under a single strategic plan.

Typically, a business is supported by a single SBU only when its scale is sufficient to justify this. Once established, an SBU has a designated accountable leader and key executives who are responsible for formulating its business strategy and overseeing and coordinating its execution. SBU heads need not "own" all organizational elements and resources required for strategy implementation.

Many of these can be purchased or subcontracted within or outside the organization. But once established, an SBU must formulate its own formal strategic plan, and its leaders are then held accountable for its performance.

Operating Units

OUs are defined typically by physical facilities or geographic areas. They contain the operating systems that must execute the SBUs' strategies (Chapter 3). OU management is responsible and accountable for formulating and executing operating plans that address the changes required within the organization to ensure successful achievement of a business' strategic objectives.

Ideally, a single OU is dedicated to support the execution of a single SBU's business strategy. However, the history of organizations and their growth seldom results in such tidiness. Often, an OU implements the strategies of more than one SBU. Thus there should be a distinct operating plan to support each strategic plan. Conversely, when a single SBU has multiple facilities and locations (recall the truck axle manufacturer in Chapter 3), its strategic plan often depends for its execution on several operating plans.

A special case of an OU is a corporate function providing supporting services to all SBUs and OUs in a large organization. These functions provide services to internal customers in areas such as human resources, finance and accounting, information technology and services, legal, and environmental services. A centralized research and development and engineering function may also be treated as an OU. Such large corporate functions are found typically in giant, multi-business organizations.

Whether an OU has its own distinct operating plan depends on both its scale and uniqueness (in terms of technology, business processes, etc.). Any facility or location with more than 50 employees is probably sufficiently sizeable to justify designation as an OU with its own operating plan. Smaller facilities/locations (e.g. fast food outlets, retail stores, bank branches, etc.) may be grouped into districts or regions for which geographically-based operating plans would be formulated.

3. The CEO's Provisional Strategic Guidelines

A third element of SONG is an explicit, formal, several-page statement by the CEO. In this document s/he outlines *personal* expectations of the strategic objectives desired of the business within a particular timeframe. S/he comments on any preferred strategies, attractive opportunities and serious threats. S/he notes any constraints on future plans. S/he lists any issues of concern.

It is crucial that the CEO position the strategic guideline statement as *provisional*, subject to later reconsideration after proposed plans have been formulated. This is another example of the need to regard the strategy formulation process as iterative. If the organization comprises more than 25–30 members, the CEO may lack a thorough understanding of the reality of business and operational details. For example, the CEO's notions about desired objectives may be romantic because the organization lacks capabilities to achieve these. Conversely, the CEO may be underestimating what the organization can realistically accomplish. Only after managers close to day-to-day realities of the business and operations formulate a proposed plan, will the CEO be able to validate (or modify) the strategic guidelines and the business strategy (see the discussion of congruency of objectives in Chapter 4).

The CEO may or may not participate directly and actively in formulating a strategic plan for a business. If s/he is not part of the Planning Group (PG, see Chapter 3), any resultant strategic plan is a *proposal*. It does not become an accepted plan until the CEO has reviewed and validated it. When the CEO is a member of the PG, validation occurs in real time as the work proceeds. In this case the resultant product is not a proposal, but rather a true plan.

The CEO's Provisional Strategic Guidelines launches the periodic cycle of SONG. It lets everyone in management know what are the CEO's agenda and concerns and expectations of them. Thus, as they begin to formulate a strategic business plan, they have a framework to stimulate their thinking about key strategic issues and choice of options. Because this framework is provisional, however, it is not a constraint to their deliberations. It is merely a starting point, something against which they can push back.

When any group of senior and middle-level managers work in a PG to formulate a proposed strategy for a business, they need to know the leader's aspirations, expectations, agenda and concerns. Without this understanding, they risk being adrift. Forced to make assumptions, they may over or underestimate what the leader really wants and expects. Or they might overlook entirely some critical consideration, because their perspective may be more narrowly focused than that of the CEO.

Here is a checklist of the kinds of topics a CEO might include in a Provisional Strategic Guideline Statement.

- key assumptions and compelling facts about the external environment
- the kind of organization we want to be (incorporated in the mission statement)
- our values, beliefs and heritage

- recent financial and other performance results (5-year review and trends)
- where we should look for future performance improvements
- sources of funds
- mission, objectives, goals and priorities
- constraints, limits and givens
- our posture towards various stake-holders and constituencies
- risks and concerns
- our capabilities … organizational strengths and weaknesses
- issues in need of resolution

In a single-business organization, the CEO makes any revisions to the provisional strategic guidelines after reviewing and validating the proposed strategic plan. As these are typically incorporated into the final version of the strategic plan, there is no need for the CEO to reissue a revised set of strategic guidelines. This is not the case in multi-business organizations. In Chapter 8, I discuss some additional features required in the CEO's Provisional Strategic Guidelines for multi-business organizations, along with the need for a Definitive Strategic Guideline Statement issued subsequently.

4. Base Future Scenario

A fourth element of SONG is a Base Future Scenario (or alternative future scenarios). These scenarios focus on the organization's external environment. They describe probable future trends in the organization's industry and markets, and in the broader social-political-economic-technological environment. If alternative scenarios are developed, these are typically "best case", "worst case" and "most probable case".

A base scenario serves three purposes. One is to make explicit and consistent for everyone in the organization, management's assumptions about future external developments. Another purpose is to examine and illuminate underlying causes for these probable future developments. This is so that managers will be sensitized to plausible future events that might impact the organization's progress toward achieving its strategic objectives (both positively and adversely). The third purpose of a base scenario is to uncover opportunities for management to take new strategic initiatives in the near-term, and to be alert to the need for mid-course corrections in its execution of the business strategy.

A base scenario is not an attempt to predict the future. This is a job for seers and fortune-tellers. Yogi Berra, American baseball's noted philosopher, once commented, "Make no forecasts, especially about the future." Rather, scenarios are an attempt to identify and analyze external strategic opportunities and imperatives by considering different plausible futures for the organization's industry. These alternative futures are developed from an understanding of current industry trends stemming from industry research, as discussed in Chapter 3.

For example, a financial institution might consider quite different industry futures to be almost equally plausible ... deregulation and re-regulation, or fragmentation and consolidation. A small team of 5–8 managers and technical specialists selected for their industry knowledge and creative imagination would then construct possible chains of events that would lead to each credible outcome. These events could be political, social, economic, demographic, technological or foreign. Each could be signaled by imagined headlines in future newspapers or business publications.

The scenario team then ponders each headline and tries to answer three questions. How credible is the event signaled by the headline? How likely is such an event to occur? If the event does occur, how significant (positive or negative) is its impact on the organization? The discussion stimulated by this process uncovers latent assumptions, draws out people's knowledge, flushes out issues, helps guide further research, exposes inconsistencies and is rich in bringing out new options. It can also help bring together different viewpoints by clarifying "where people are coming from".

After several working sessions, the scenario team documents (in no more than a few pages) a proposed base scenario (or two or three alternative scenarios) for the entire PG to consider and discuss (see following section). This occurs early in the process of formulating a strategic plan, so that the insights gained will illuminate the PG's subsequent analyses of the current situation and choice of strategic options.

Beyond serving as a key input into the strategic planning process, the base scenario also serves three additional purposes once implementation of the strategy begins. It is a monitoring device to check on the external developments that actually occur. It is an early warning system, alerting management to possible subsequent developments in a projected chain. And it is a device for managing uncertainties that are often ignored because they are "beyond anyone's control".

Once developed, a base scenario should be regarded not as a finished product but rather as a working document, subject to continuous reassessment and modification. Its value stems less from the document itself and more from the *process* of its initial development and subsequent review and updating. The resultant insights and sensitivities gained facilitate prompt strategic and organizational adaptation when outside forces begin to undermine the business or the organization.

5. An SBU's Strategic Business Plan

A strategic business plan is a key element of SONG. In a single business organization, this foundation document serves two different functions. Its formulation is the means by which management decides where to focus its efforts and allocate resources over a several year period. It is also a directional statement to inform the rest of the organization, customers, suppliers, shareholders, funders and other stake-holders. This statement (in full or summary) should be shared with everyone interested and concerned about management's future intentions and plans for carrying them out, so that they will understand and support management's efforts. In multi-business organizations, discussed in Chapters 8 and 9, the SBU's strategic plan serves several additional purposes.

The focus of a strategic business plan is primarily external to the organization ... on markets, customers, competitors, suppliers, funders and regulators. The principal question addressed is "What do we want to achieve in the marketplace, and how will we do this?" A secondary focus is internal, addressing the question, "What changes do we need to make within the organization to support what we want to accomplish in the marketplace?"

The time horizon for a strategic business plan is several years ... from 3–7, depending on how slow or fast moving are the changes occurring in the organization's industry. In exceptionally dynamic industries, where developments are taking place at a rapid rate (e.g. semiconductors, financial services, telecommunications, entertainment), strategic plans need to be reviewed and reformulated more frequently than in industries that are more stable and slow-changing (e.g. mining, basic chemicals, agriculture, furniture, basic food products).

Process Issues in Plan Formulation

The literature on strategic plans and how to formulate them is extensive (1). Most of what has been published is concerned with *content* ... what a good strategic plan should address and contain. There is no need here to duplicate what is already available. I do, however, want to discuss several fundamental aspects of the strategic planning *process* which in my view are crucial to achieving a sound, high quality plan that is subsequently executed successfully. A superb plan that sits in a credenza, unrealized in effective implementation, is both useless and represents wasted resources.

The task of formulating a strategic plan should not be confined to a small group of top-level executives. This all too common practice occurs because top managers in most organizations regard strategic planning as *their* exclusive domain. They believe that only they have the requisite broad perspective and vision. Although there may be some truth in this view, there are several serious associated risks, all of which can undermine the soundness of the plan and the likelihood of its successful execution.

One risk is that top-level managers may lack sufficient current understanding of what is going on in the organization's external environment ... especially recent industry, market and customer trends and developments, and competitor information. Similarly, these senior executives may be so remote from the day-to-day details of internal operations that their assumptions about the organization's capabilities may be unfounded or wrong. A third risk is that conclusions and strategic choices based on flawed analyses will result in a plan lacking in credibility to those who are key to its execution. When middle- and lower-level managers and supervisors view a plan as unrealistic, open to question or unsound, they cannot be counted on to "buy-in" and proceed enthusiastically with implementation. Even a sound plan may appear unconvincing to those uninvolved in its formulation because they do not understand (or believe) the rationale underlying the choices made. The consequence in both instances is lack of commitment to implementing the plan, and execution that falls short of desired results.

All these risks can be minimized when the group assigned to formulate the plan is considerably larger and broader than a handful of top executives. I believe that an effective Planning Group (PG) formed to develop a strategic business plan should include all senior- and middle-level managers (plus some representative first-line supervisors and key employees) who meet at least one of two criteria:

1. ability to contribute substantive information about key aspects of the business, its industry, markets, customers, competitors, funders and/or about the organization and operational details; and

2. have the power and influence to play an important role in executing the plan.

A PG might also include individuals outside the organization who represent important sources of knowledge and influence. These might be members of the organization's Board of Directors (or Advisers), especially in not-for-profit organizations, key customers, funders, distributors and suppliers. A constraint may be willingness to invest the time and effort required of a PG member. Another constraint may be perceived conflicts of interest.

An effective PG may have 15–30 members. Typically, 3–4 levels of management and every organizational function and department key to the business are represented, wherever they are located in the organization. A properly constituted

PG when working, will have in the room collectively all knowledge and insights needed to perform analyses, draw sound conclusions and make high quality strategic choices.

Such a PG also ensures that all managers key to successful plan execution, because they have participated fully in formulating the plan, understand it and the reasoning underlying the choices made. Furthermore, by the conclusion of the plan formulation process they believe in and have bought into the outcome. Thus, there will be a critical mass of managers to launch execution with a high degree of understanding, commitment and enthusiasm. These are crucial for achieving desired outcomes because key knowledge can be communicated widely to address questions and concerns, and positive "can-do" attitudes enable inevitable unforeseen problems and obstacles to be surmounted.

Throughout the plan formulation process, an effective PG achieves two objectives concurrently. One is to draw conclusions and make choices that are sound and realistic. The other objective is to achieve consensus.

Although all PG members come from the same organization, by no means do they begin work together with a shared set of understandings, assumptions and opinions. Quite the contrary. The cognitive and emotional baggage they bring with them to the PG is shaped and colored by their own unique specialized knowledge and experiences both of the business and of those parts of the organization with which they have been involved.

How then, can a PG, especially when large, ever achieve consensus in making sound choices? A combination of six factors makes such an outcome possible. One is access to comprehensive, valid information about the organization, its internal operations, and its external environment. Another is buy-in to that information by everyone in the group, so that each finds it credible. Third, it is vital that a PG focus *initially* on understanding the *external* environment. This is crucial because the external world is less familiar than the internal, and because it is easier to be more objective in discussing externals than internals. Most important, the external realities provide a framework, inform discussions and drive the choices made throughout the plan formulation process.

A fourth factor contributing to sound consensus, is assigning *appropriate* tasks to the PG. Large groups can be effective in critiquing, discussing and validating presented materials, performing analyses and reaching conclusions requiring deductive reasoning. They are far less effective in tasks requiring creative thought. Any creative work should be assigned to small groups of six or less (2).

Two additional factors contribute to sound consensus. The group must have a structured, disciplined agenda led by someone skilled in group process (3), employing analytical instruments or tools designed for group applications (4). Whenever the group meets as a whole, they should do so for substantial, sustained periods of time, at least a full day and preferably two. This provides sufficient time to establish and sustain a working climate and momentum supportive to working effectively together.

When all six of these factors are applied in a large PG, each member replaces areas of ignorance, misconception and bias with more accurate and comprehensive pictures of external and internal reality. These pictures are shared within the group and constitute a common information base. Subsequent analyses and interpretations of this information within a framework of common criteria result in a mental model shared by the PG. Such a model greatly facilitates the achievement of consensus.

Formulating a Plan: Selecting the Foundation Strategies

When a PG formulates a strategic plan, there are two distinct phases. The first concludes with a provisional choice of a limited number of strategies. These are the foundation of the plan and define its thrust and direction. In the second phase, the work required to implement each strategy is specified in the form of discrete tasks, along with accountabilities, timetables and resources needed. Also, a process is defined for measuring, monitoring and communicating implementation progress and accomplishments. All this constitutes the superstructure of the plan that conveys to everyone concerned its true nature and meaning.

Note that strategy selection cannot be considered firm until the supporting action plans are developed and validated in terms of the practicability of resources required. Hence, the initial choice of strategies marking the end of Phase I must be considered provisional until validated by the formulation and assessment of the supporting action program. This is another example of the need to view the process of strategy formulation as iterative rather than linear.

The number of generic strategic options for any SBU in any industry (profit, not-for-profit or government) is finite ... no more than 19 (see Appendix B). No strategic plan should be based on more than 3–5 distinct strategies. To attempt more would lose the focus so essential for successful execution. Selecting which particular strategies to pursue in a plan from the 19 generic options depends on achieving the best fit among four areas of consideration. One is the nature of the organization's external environment (characteristics of the industry, markets, competition, etc., discussed in Chapter 3). Another is the nature of the organization itself and its operating characteristics (people, processes. policies and procedures, structure, technology, etc., also discussed in Chapter 3). This is articulated in an assessment of organizational capabilities or strengths and weaknesses. A third consideration is the strategic objectives desired by the leadership, articulated in the CEO's Provisional Strategic Guideline Statement. And the fourth consideration is which 3–5 strategies should be pursued. The better the fit among these, the more sound will be the plan and the more probable will be management's success in executing it. Only by treating the strategy formulation process as iterative can best fit be achieved.

In its choice of 3–5 strategies, a PG is most likely to achieve consensus when there is *prior* agreement on two factors (external realities and organizational capabilities), and consideration of a third. This third factor is the desired mission and strategic objectives offered by the CEO in his/her Provisional Strategic Guideline Statement (Section 3 of this chapter). Although these objectives have not yet been established concretely and accepted at this stage in the planning process, they nevertheless suggest a direction and order of magnitude of desired achievement.

In that light, the PG considers the compelling facts about the organization and its external environment ... those characteristics and trends most relevant to management's aspirations (also embodied in the base scenario). In the external environment these are "givens", beyond management's reach. Yet they form the backdrop for strategy formulation. As it ponders the compelling facts, the PG identifies and prioritizes a set of 4–6 *key strategic issues* (KSIs). These are the most important questions or problems which the PG believes must be addressed in the strategic plan.

Selecting KSIs is a task requiring both creative imagination and analytical thinking. It is most effectively done in small groups. At this point in the strategy formulation process, the PG is broken out into several small (4–6 member) groups. Each group collectively develops several posters (on flip chart paper).

A poster is comprised of an array of validated 3X5 cards used to describe the organization and its external environment (see Chapter 3). The particular cards selected for the array are perceived by the group as related in some way (cause/effect, influence/outcome, etc.). Arrows are drawn showing relationships, and a caption is inscribed that communicates the intended significance or meaning of the array.

All posters are then viewed by the PG as in an art show. Each PG member then writes on 3 blank 3X5 cards her/his individual conclusion about the three most pressing issues or problems confronting the organization (one issue per card). S/he then prioritizes these. Each PG member in turn then reads out to the entire PG his/her top priority issue. This is recorded on a flip chart. Duplications are noted. This process is repeated for the second and third priority issues. By the end of this process, it is apparent which 5–6 issues are the most widespread urgent choices. Not only have the KSIs been identified, but also consensus has been achieved on both issue and priority.

The other factor requiring PG agreement before strategy selection, is an assessment of the organization's performance capabilities. This stems from an analysis of the organization's nature and operating characteristics, typically expressed as *strengths and weaknesses*. Remember that no organizational characteristic is *inherently* a strength or a weakness. Any characteristic is a true strength or weakness only relative to competitors' characteristics, and in light of intended objectives. Unlike the characteristics of the external environment which are givens, management can change organizational performance. It can amplify a strength and eliminate, lessen or offset a weakness. Accomplishing this, however, usually takes considerable time ... sometimes months but more often, years.

As the process of identifying strengths and weaknesses is essentially analytical, this task is performed by the PG working together as a whole. PG members are asked first to reflect (without discussion) and write down individually their conclusions about strengths and weaknesses. Nominations are then invited for recording on flip charts. These are then discussed by the full group prior to final validation.

By reflecting on the key strategic issues, the organization's strengths and weaknesses and the CEO's proposed mission and objectives, each PG member forms a mental model. This model enables members to identify criteria for screening generic strategic options for appropriateness or best fit. While external realities are givens and organizational capabilities are susceptible to change over time, both objectives and strategies are immediately variable. Managers can test various options until a best fit is achieved.

Once it has agreed on a prioritized set of KSIs and on an analysis of the organization's strengths and weaknesses, a large PG can reach consensus on selecting 3–5 strategies within several hours. As with KSIs, choice of proposed strategies requires both creativity and analysis. This is best done in small groups of 4–6 members. When the PG is broken out into small groups, each is asked to propose a set of up to four strategies that will together address the KSIs and provisional objectives, in light of the strengths and weaknesses. Each group is also asked to note on flip charts, the most important elements of each proposed strategy. When the PG reconvenes, each group presents its proposals. From subsequent discussion, consensus is reached on up to five strategies.

The preceding work of discussing the business definition, the CEO' Provisional Strategic Guidelines (especially mission and objectives), validating the compelling facts about the organization and its external environment, identifying and prioritizing the KSIs and analyzing the organization's strengths and weaknesses will require a PG to devote about 12–18 hours or up to two full days (see Figure 4 for an overview of the plan formulation process). The amount of time depends on the size and complexity of the organization and its business(es).

Formulating a Plan: Developing the Superstructure

Once a PG selects 3–5 foundation strategies, its choices should be regarded as provisional. Not until it has described the actual work required to execute these strategies, along with the necessary resources (including time), can it feel confident that the strategies initially identified are in fact practicable. Should the PG find that its initial choices will take far longer to implement than it envisioned, or that the organization lacks or cannot afford the resources required, the PG should reconsider its choice of strategies. Alternatively, it might revise the objectives. Again, this illustrates the necessarily iterative nature of the entire process.

A fundamental reason to incorporate detailed action plans into a strategic plan, is to validate the initial choice of strategies. Another major purpose is to outline a roadmap for implementation. This roadmap should specify for each strategy: (a) a sequence of tasks that describe the scope of the work to be done and the intended "deliverable" or outcome for each task; (b) the resources needed to perform each task; (c) who is accountable for each task; and (d) a timetable including projected start and completion dates for each task.

Such an action program is the principal element in a strategic plan's superstructure. It serves to inform everyone involved in executing the plan and those impacted by it: (a) what is truly intended by the plan; (b) what changes are likely; and (c) what expectations are being made of the organization and its members. The action program is also the basis for the implementation measurement and monitoring process described in Section 7 of this chapter.

A key issue in formulating an action program is what level of detail is appropriate. In specifying the sequence of work tasks required to execute a strategy, the potential for detailed elaboration is almost endless. Inevitably, any initial effort to describe a work plan will result in some tasks that are substantial in scope, requiring many months to complete, and others that are more narrow and focused. This does not matter, so long as the major elements of the strategy are identified and addressed. Later on, a leader with accountability for a broad scope task can as a first step, lead her/his team in formulating a more detailed action plan for completing that task. This process is in fact beneficial because it serves to foster understanding of and generate buy-in and commitment to task accomplishment by the team. As a guideline, each strategy in the strategic plan should be supported by an action plan of about 7–14 tasks.

A strategic plan's superstructure includes seven other elements. Two are processes for measuring and monitoring accomplishments and progress in executing the strategic plan (see Section 7). Another is assumptions about future events outside management's control which are key to successful execution of the strategic plan. Another is a list of the major qualitative changes to the organization expected to result from successful plan execution. A fourth element is an analysis of risk of implementation failure. The sixth element is a plan for communicating the plan and its subsequent implementation achievements and progress within the organization and to any appropriate external stake-holders (see Section 10). The seventh element is a projection of the financial impact of the plan on the organization.

When a strategic plan includes explicit statements about key future assumptions, expected changes and an analysis of risk, these serve as useful points of reference later on throughout the process for monitoring implementation. Together, these statements clarify the thinking of the PG when it formulated the plan. During the several-years of implementation when unanticipated changes occur within the organization and/or in its external environment (as they inevitably do), managers who monitor plan execution can raise important questions. "What original assumptions are no longer valid?" "Have we seen any evidence that expected changes are occurring?" "Would the original risk analysis still hold today?" Answer to these questions will determine what, if any, modifications are needed to the action program (Section 7). I call these three plan elements signal generators.

The PG's process for developing the superstructure for the strategic plan is somewhat different from that used to select the foundation strategies. In Phase 1 of the strategic plan formulation process, the PG works together as a whole to discuss and validate mission and objectives, business definition, and compelling facts about the organization and its external environment. It also works as a whole to assess the organization's performance capabilities and in the final stages of identifying and prioritizing KSIs and selecting the foundation strategies. All these tasks require critical analysis and deductive reasoning ... work that a large group can do effectively. When more creative thinking is needed, as in initial efforts to identify KSIs and to choose foundation strategies, small groups of PG members are formed to work for brief periods. The PG as a whole then responds and integrates the conclusions reached by the small groups.

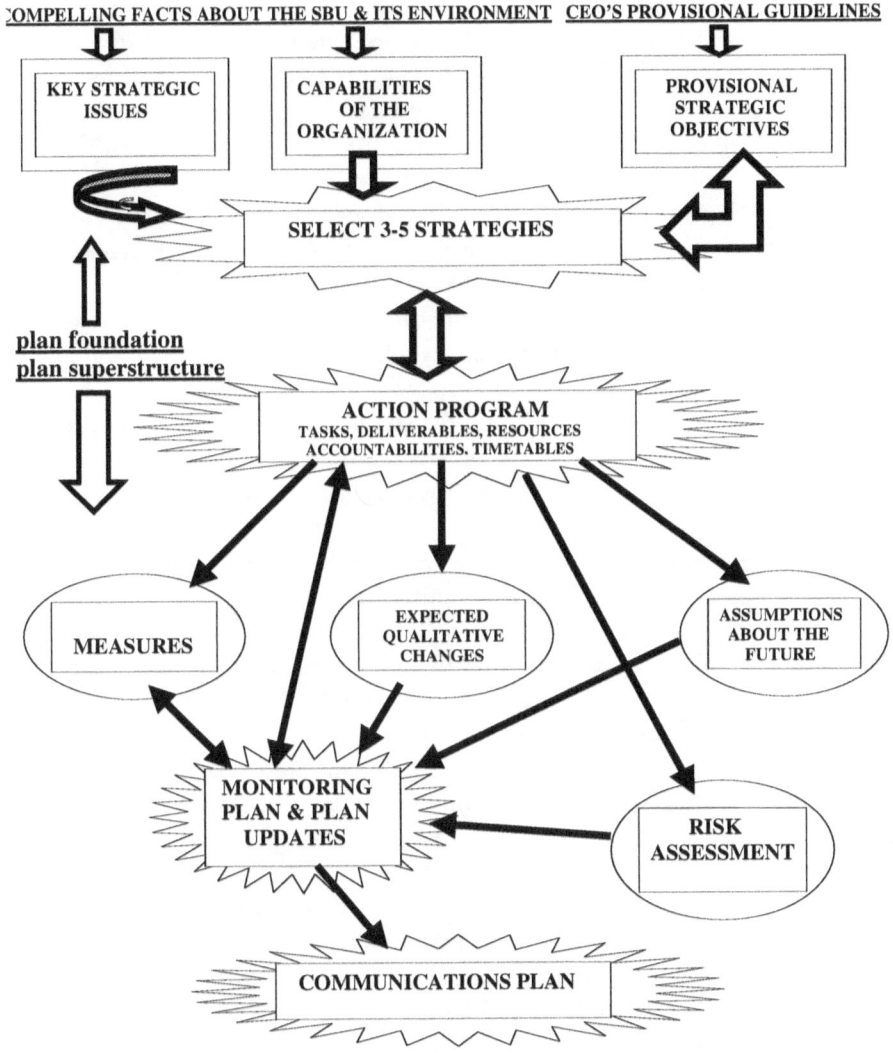

Figure 4
STRATEGIC BUSINESS PLAN FORMULATION PROCESS

Formulating an action program is the principal task in developing a plan's superstructure. This work requires much creative thinking ... something accomplished better by small groups. For each provisional foundation strategy selected in Phase 1, a small (5–8 members) Action Planning Group (APG) is designated, led by a member of the PG (the other APG members may or may not be PG members, and should be selected for their ability to make relevant, knowledgeable and creative inputs). Each APG is charged to specify a *proposed* sequence of 7–14 tasks, which when completed, will have executed the assigned strategy. An APG's proposed action plan outlines each task, its intended deliverable or outcome and notes any required resources including estimated time required to complete the task. Typically, in the interval between the PG's meetings, an APG meets for 2–3 half-day sessions to complete this task 5.

Formulating a proposed action plan is best done by considering first how one might describe the organization and business *after the strategy is successfully executed.* The APG develops a single flip chart with a list of statements describing how the organization and business will function in the future (desired outcomes). Next the APG specifies the critical changes required to achieve these outcomes, along with what specific actions are required to trigger these changes (e.g. a study, management decision, redesign of a product, service or process, etc.). Finally, the APG describes the kind and scope of work required to achieve the desired changes and outcomes. This last step is the basis for articulating the tasks comprising the proposed action plan required to execute the proposed strategy. Once the tasks are described, the APG identifies each task's end point (deliverable) and estimates the resources required to accomplish this.

The APGs' proposed action plans are then presented to the full PG for critique, modification and validation. After the PG has agreed and validated all task descriptions, a small group of the PG's most senior-level executives meets to formulate an integrated action program that reflects their notion of priorities and accountabilities. Referring to the APGs' estimates and notes about resources, this top-level group establishes start and completion dates for each task and assigns accountabilities. The integrated action program is then presented to the PG for final review and validation.

Other elements of the superstructure (elements 12–17 listed on page 91 in the section "The Completed Strategic Plan") are developed after the PG validates all action tasks. This work is done by the PG as a whole. Typically, working with inputs from APGs, a PG can develop the entire superstructure for a strategic plan in 8–16 hours (depending on the size and complexity of the organization and its business(es).

Additional Plan Elements Relevant to Plan Implementation

After the PG validates the action program, it completes the strategic plan by formulating seven additional plan elements (12–17 below), all of which are crucial to successful plan execution. The two most critical, Measures and a Monitoring Process (13 and 14 below) are discussed later at length in Section 7 of this Chapter. The Communications Plan (12 below) is discussed in Section 11 of this Chapter. The remaining four elements are described below.

Signal Generators

The purpose served by articulating Key Assumptions, Major Changes Expected and Risk Analysis (15–17 below) is to establish an explicit statement of conditions relevant to the time when the plan was first formulated. These conditions support the rationale for the plan. Later on, as the plan is implemented, should these conditions change, signals are generated alerting management to consider the possibility that the plan may need to be modified.

The plan element, Key Assumptions, is a list of assumptions made by the PG at the time of plan formulation about factors typically external to the organization and beyond management's control or influence. If such a factor has the potential for invalidating or derailing the plan, it should be listed. For example, key assumptions might be: "no burdensome legislation, regulation or litigation"; "continued commitment and support by our board of directors and other stakeholders"; "reasonable continuity of leadership". The underlying premise for the list of key assumptions is that each assumption must hold for the duration of plan implementation in order for the plan to remain as written and to be successfully executed. Key Assumptions are developed by inviting the PG to nominate, discuss and validate items for the list.

The plan element, Major Changes Expected, is a list of all the aspects of organizational characteristics and performance that are expected to change as a consequence of executing the strategic plan. Items on this list are typically qualitative. They augment the quantitative measures listed in plan element 13, Indicators and Measures of Improvement and Achievement. The list of Expected Changes is developed by reviewing the action program and answering the question, "If we succeed in completing these action steps, what visible evidence can we expect in terms of improvements in how things work within the organization?" Expected Changes are developed by inviting the PG to nominate, discuss and validate items for the list.

Analysis of Risk refers to the risk of failure to implement the plan. There are eight different factors of risk to consider:

1. probability that the key assumptions will hold throughout the period required for plan execution ... the higher the probability, the lower the risk;

2. ambitiousness of the strategic objectives ... the greater the ambitiousness (or stretch), the higher the risk;

3. familiarity of the strategies selected for the plan to management ... the more familiar and experienced management is with the strategies, the lower the risk;

4. management's past track record in implementing plans of any kind ... the more successful management has been in past plan implementation efforts, the lower the risk;

5. overall management competence in managing the organization ... the higher the competence, the lower the risk;

6. depth in management back-up ... the greater this depth (number of lower-level managers able and ready to fill higher level positions), the lower the risk;

7. organization's responsiveness to management's efforts to introduce changes ... the greater this responsiveness, the lower the risk;

8. conflict of the changes required by the strategic plan with the existing culture of the organization ... the greater the conflict, the higher the risk.

The PG estimates the level of risk that management will fail to implement the plan successfully on a scale of high-medium-low. PG members are invited to register their individual estimates by voting on each of the eight factors listed above. Votes are noted on a grid shown on a flip chart. Once this done, an estimate of overall risk can be determined.

Financial Summary

The final element of the strategic plan is a financial summary of the projected impact of the plan on the organization's finances. This is done by a small group led by the senior financial manager/executive on the PG. This group does its work in the interval between the PG's working session when it validates the proposed action plans and develops the other elements of the superstructure, and its final working session when it reviews and validates the draft strategic plan document. The projected financial summary is prepared in parallel with the proposed timetable and accountability assignments for the action program, and is submitted to the PG for validation in its final working session (see below).

The financial summary is developed by considering each action step specified in the action program. Estimates are made of the likelihood of any income stemming from successful completion of that action step, along with any probable costs incurred. Also, the probability and financial implications of achieving the strategic objectives are factored in.

The Completed Strategic Plan

The final product of both phases of the strategic planning process is a document comprised of 18 distinct elements:

1. Executive Summary

2. Key characteristics (compelling facts and trends) about the relevant industry and market(s) or segments thereof

3. Key characteristics of relevant competitors, competitive dynamics, key success factors, and organization's current competitive position

4. Key characteristics (compelling facts) about the organization, including core competencies and capabilities

5. Key strategic issues (prioritized)

6. Analysis of the organization's capabilities (strengths and weaknesses)

7. Summary of the organization's past/current strategies and performance

8. Statements of vision, mission and values

9. Business definition

10. Strategic objectives, boundary conditions (constraints) and strategies

11. Action programs supporting strategies

12. Communications plan

13. Indicators and measures of improvement and achievement

14. Monitoring process

15. Key assumptions (on which successful execution depends)

16. Major changes expected

17. Risk analysis

18. Financial summary: resultant performance projected and resources needed

Before the strategic plan document is published and disseminated, the PG should review it in draft form. This enables PG members to examine the entire document, check it for accuracy, clarity, consistency and completeness. Also, they have an opportunity for second thoughts about conclusions reached and choices made. This painstaking review and discussion takes 3–6 hours and typically yields a document of improved quality. This process also reinforces and enhances PG members' understanding of and buy-in to the plan and strengthens their commitment to successful execution.

In its final review of the completed (draft) strategic plan, the PG applies the following criteria to assess and test the quality of its work product:

- Does the overall plan reflect an *external perspective*? To what extent are analyses and conclusions *driven* by an understanding of external realities?

- How *comprehensive and valid* are the basic data about the organization and its external environment?

- To what extent were the conclusions reached and choices made based on *objective* consideration?

- Are the key strategic issues *addressed*?

- To what extent are the action plans *comprehensive, clear and explicit*?

- How *congruent* are key strategic issues, organizational strengths and weaknesses, competitive position, resources, objectives and strategies?

- How *realistic* are key assumptions, expected changes and analysis of risk?

6. Operating Plan(s)

Typically, the thrust of an SBU's strategic plan focuses on the organization's relationship to its external environment … its markets, customers, industry, competitors, funders, other external stakeholders, etc. The plan describes changes that the organization wants to achieve in these relationships, and how it intends to accomplish these. Thus a strategic plan (particularly the action program) is concerned primarily with how the organization will enter new and retain or improve its position in existing markets, acquire new and retain existing customers and funders, and form new and strengthen existing external alliances and relationships. Some of the plan may be concerned with improving existing and introducing new offerings (products and services) to customers.

In order for an organization to succeed in achieving any of the above, it must often make some changes *internally* to its operating systems (see Chapter 3). These changes may be addressed in one of the strategic plan's foundation strategies. If the organization is relatively small (fewer than 100 members) and operating in a single facility, the action plan supporting the strategic plan's internal strategy may be sufficient to guide the change effort. But if the organization is larger, and/or is operating in multiple locations and facilities, an effective SONG requires one or more separate operating plans to support a single strategic plan (recall the examples in Chapter 3: the organization producing truck axles; fast food and retail chains; and large support functions in giant organizations; also the discussion in this chapter of Operating Units (OU) in Section 2).

Like a strategic plan, an operating plan, is a key element of SONG. This foundation document serves six functions. Its formulation is the means by which management decides where to focus its *internal* efforts and allocate resources over the near-term. It is also a directional statement that specifies for everyone within the organization with an interest in the implementation of the strategy, the work that must be done to execute the strategic plan. Third, an operating plan is a means for involving all key players in the operating system(s) that support the business, in the execution of the business strategy … ensuring their understanding and commitment to the plan. Fourth, an operating plan is the basis for an effective measurement, monitoring and plan updating process, a key to ensuring successful implementation. Fifth, operating plans are the basis for budgets. And sixth, an operating plan is the starting point for effective ongoing communications about the strategic plan and its execution.

The time horizon for an operating plan is about half that of a strategic plan … 2–3 years.

This is because managements' efforts are focused entirely within the organization. With a strategic plan, management tries to change the relationship of its organization to its industry, markets, customers, funders and competitors … entities that may be influenced somewhat, but are well beyond management's direct control. Accomplishing any changes takes a long time. Within the organization, where management has more direct and immediate leverage, changes can be achieved faster.

Operating and Strategic Plans: Similarities and Differences

The literature on operating plans and how to formulate them is sparse (6). In my experience, I have found little consistency in how operating plans are defined and applied in actual practice. Some organizations treat operating plans simply as short-term versions of their strategic plan, with a 1–2 year (rather than 5) horizon. In other organizations, the operating plan is little more than a set of numbers detailing the near-term financial implications of the business strategy. Such plans spell out the resources required to implement the strategic plan over the initial year or two, along with quantitative forecasts of performance improvement. In this approach, an operating plan is much like a budget.

In my view, an operating plan is very much like a strategic plan both in content and in the way it is formulated. However there are some important differences:

1. A strategic plan is aimed at improving or changing the organization's position and performance *externally* in its industry and marketplace; an operating plan is *subsidiary* to the strategic plan and is aimed at changing *internally* how the organization's operating systems work so that they better support the strategic plan and ensure successful execution.

2. As with a strategic plan, formulating an operating plan is driven by understanding the operating system's *externals*. In this instance, these are the thrust of the strategic plan and its underlying rationale, and the resultant demands made by the business strategies on the supporting operating system(s). Examples of these demands are lower total *costs*, more reliable or more responsive *delivery* of products and services to the marketplace, better *quality* of market offerings, and better, more responsive *market offerings* brought more rapidly to the marketplace.

3. As with a strategic plan, an operating plan should be formulated by an (Operational) Planning Group (OPG) made up of 12–30 key players in the operating system addressed by the operating plan. These are mostly middle- and lower-level department managers plus a few representative first-line supervisors … people with intimate knowledge of operations who have the power to execute the required changes to the operating system. Typically, the most senior manager in an OPG is the SBU head or facility (plant or office) manager (all other comments about process made in the preceding section apply here).

4. As with strategic plans, the number of generic strategies for operating plans is finite (33). Most are different from the 19 generic business strategies described in Appendix B. Generic operating plan strategies are described in Appendix C.

5. In general, the granularity or level of detail is greater in operating plans than in strategic plans. The latter are concerned with broad industry trends and market forces, neither of which lend themselves to precise characterization. Operating systems, internal to the organization, lend themselves to more accurate and detailed description and analysis. Thus, a work plan specifying how an operating system will be changed so as better to support a strategic plan, is likely to be better defined and more detailed than action plans in a strategic plan.

6. Like the plan formulation process for strategic business plans, the process for developing operating plans has the same two distinct phases. Phase 1 concludes with the selection of 3–5 foundation strategies for the operating plan (see 4 above). Phase 2 is concerned with the development of the superstructure: an action program; a process for measuring and monitoring implementation progress; key assumptions; expected changes; an analysis of risk; and a communications plan. The Phase 2 process for formulating operating and strategic plans are the same. The Phase 1 process for developing operating plans differs from that for strategic plans only in the factors requiring OPG agreement prior to their choice of foundation strategies, and the means for reaching that agreement. These differences are discussed below.

Special Aspects of the Operating Plan Formulation Process

The plan formulation process applied by an OPG in Phase 1 is very similar to that for a PG. It differs only in the specifics of the subject matter being addressed and the analyses and conclusions required to form a mental model for selecting the operating plan's foundation strategies. An OPG develops this model after achieving consensus on three factors. First is a prioritized list of *high-leverage targets* on which to focus in order to change the way the operating system works. Second is a list of *priorities for the operating system* as it supports the execution of the strategic business plan. Third is an assessment of *operating system capabilities* (see Figure 5 for an overview of the entire process for formulating an operating plan).

High-Leverage Targets

A high-leverage target is an element of an operating system (typically a process, system, policy, procedure, organizational function or department) which if impacted, has sufficient leverage to change the behavior of the entire system in a desired direction. Remember that the overriding objective of any operating plan is to improve the effectiveness of the entire operating system as it supports the execution of the strategic business plan's strategies. When management focuses on a high-leverage target and invests resources to change it, a lasting improvement will result in the effectiveness of the entire operating system. Typically, high-leverage targets are operating system elements that are dysfunctional and/or the source of widespread employee dissatisfaction and frustration. To identify these requires first a comprehensive description of the operating system as it is currently working, and then a systematic analysis of each element of that system.

For example, consider an 1800 employee division of a giant global corporation in the business of designing, manufacturing and marketing desktop work stations. The SBU's principal market offering is computer-driven systems comprised of some 50 hardware and software elements, most of which are manufactured and supplied by sister divisions in this corporation. In the SBU's strategic plan, the external environment was characterized as fast moving and intensely competitive on the bases of: (1) market offerings that meet customer needs (with software the most important consideration); (2) quality (performance and reliability); (3) price; and (4) service (delivery reliability, customer education and maintenance). The SBU's competitive position was assessed as neither leading nor weak in a group of some dozen competitors, but somewhere in the middle of the pack. Its strongest position was in the manufacturing market segment.

The thrust of this SBU's strategic plan was to improve its competitive position by gaining market share in manufacturing markets and entering and penetrating office markets. A key aspect of executing this strategy required the SBU to modify its existing product to suit the needs of the office market, and to bring this new offering to the marketplace within 18 months at a competitive price.

The SBU's past track record in designing new products and bringing them to market was unimpressive. This process was dominated by design engineers who felt certain that they knew what customers needed. These engineers had little use for inputs from the marketing department, and were oblivious to the cost implications of their design choices. The fastest time for a new product introduction had been 38 months from initial design to delivery of the first lot.

Figure 5
OPERATING PLAN FORMULATION PROCESS

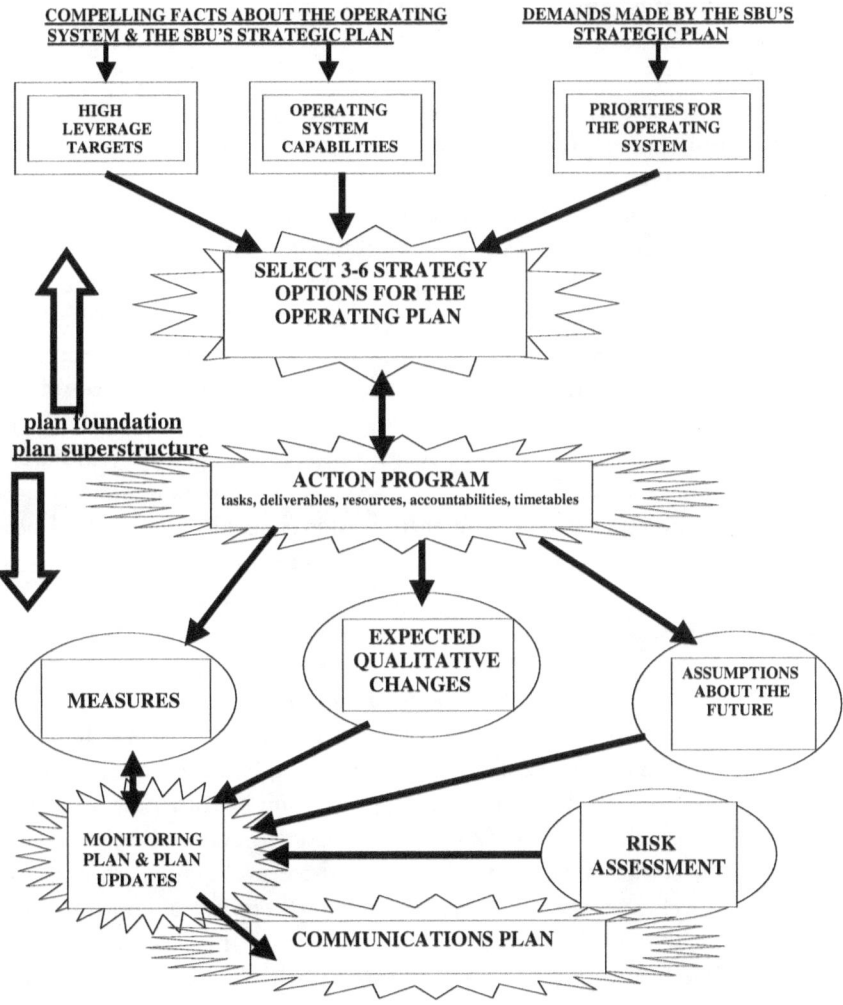

Analyzing the operating system (encompassing the entire Divisional organization and its linkages to the other company divisions supplying hardware and software components for the SBU's market offerings), the

OPG identified a high-leverage target: the process of new product design, development and introduction. This process encompassed the relationships among the Division's key functions of design engineering, marketing, manufacturing, and finance, and between the Division and other company divisions involved in selling desktop workstations and supplying components for the Division's market offerings. This process was identified as a high-leverage target because its past performance was entirely inadequate in light of the SBU's new business strategy. Not only did it take twice as long as was now necessary to bring new products to the marketplace, but also design engineering's dominance of the process was unlikely to produce products in tune with the special needs of the office market.

By focusing on improving the new product introduction process, the OPS in its operating plan could address simultaneously three issues crucial to successful execution of the business strategy. First, time required to bring new products to market would be reduced dramatically. Second, new products would be more tuned to meet customer needs because their design would reflect not only the views of design engineers, but also those of sales and marketing. Third, new products prices would be more competitive because early inputs into product designs by manufacturing and finance would lower total costs. Thus by improving one key process in the operating system, the entire system's performance would be able better to support the execution of the business strategy.

Consider another example of a high-leverage target.

A 300-member firm designs, manufactures and markets electro-mechanical devices used to actuate control surfaces that guide the flight of aircraft and missiles. For many years, sales had been flat because costs were higher than those of key competitors and because promised delivery times were often missed. Within the operating system (the entire organization) several factors contributed to these problems. Although inventory levels everywhere were excessive, there were continuous spot shortages of critical components. There were high levels of regularly scheduled overtime and rework, along with high levels of employee absenteeism and turnover.

A new strategic plan was developed to increase market share by lowering prices and improving delivery performance. In formulating its operating plan, the OPG identified the need to improve control of material flow as a high-leverage target. Improving this single process would reduce inventories, improve planning and scheduling predictability, and reduce the need for rework and overtime work. Improvement in all these areas would also reduce the underlying causes for high employee absenteeism and turnover. Total costs would also be reduced. Thus, by improving a single process, the entire operating system would perform in a way that would better support execution of the business strategy.

Operating System Priorities and Objectives

Every operating system, whether it supports a business in the profit, not-for-profit or government sectors, must be responsive to the strategic imperatives or demands made on the operating system by the business strategies in the strategic plan. These demands focus on particular aspects of the operating system's performance, and typically require improvements.

Generically, there are probably no more than seven distinct kinds of demand that a strategic plan can make on the performance of an operating system (7). One is *lower total costs*, typically to support greater flexibility in pricing products and services to gain market share, or to increase profits/surplus or to reduce debt. Another related but somewhat different demand is better *utilization of assets*. This could mean making use of idle capacity or wasted space, better planning, scheduling and layouts, better returns on investments or rentals, and better equipment utilization.

A third demand is to improve the *quality* of products and services. When customers can actually perceive and value superior quality, an organization can achieve a better position in its marketplace by improving the level of quality of its products and services. This could mean better uniformity and reliability, or user friendliness, or longer product life, or appearance, or reduced need for maintenance and repair, or more effective perceived outcomes.

A fourth demand is greater *flexibility in changing market offerings*. This means improving the operating system's responsiveness to market requirements for innovations in products and services as well as faster introduction of these changes (recall the example of the work station SBU described earlier in this section).

The remaining three generic demands that a business strategy might make on an operating system all have to do with various aspects of the system's ability to deliver its market offerings to customers. One is improving the system's ability to *meet delivery commitments* reliably and predictably. Another is increasing the system's capability for *highly responsive delivery*. This means improving performance in meeting very rapidly, customers' unscheduled and unanticipated requirements for products and services. The last generic demand is improving the operating system's *flexibility in changing volume* or capacity (up or down). This means improving responsiveness in meeting needs for growth or reduction, including cyclical and seasonal changes.

Typically, for any strategic plan, only two or three of these seven generic demands or imperatives are paramount. An OPG must identify these and make them explicit. In my experience, few organizations make such an analysis. Managers are often unaware of the implications of the strategic business plan for their department or function. Left to their own assumptions, they allow the traditional values held within their function or department to determine priorities. Thus, sales managers generally assume that sales and revenues are the highest priority, engineering managers regard innovation and technical excellence as paramount, marketing managers are concerned primarily with market share and meeting customer needs, financial and manufacturing managers are concerned with costs, human services program managers are concerned with improving the quality of life for their clients, service program managers are concerned with service quality and client satisfaction, and so on.

> For example, a division of a leading U.S. manufacturer of electrical products for the kitchen was experiencing an erosion of its market position. The division's strategic objective was to regain and increase share of a very competitive market. In its strategic plan, the division defined its business as near-commodity, with price the most important basis of competition. The strategic plan called for more aggressive product pricing, based on reducing total costs.
>
> Within the division, however, two current programs were demanding substantial investment. One aimed at developing new features for the product. The other was a comprehensive effort to upgrade product and service quality. The effect of both these initiatives was to *increase* costs ... an outcome directly at odds with the business strategy. Erosion of market share continued.

Clearly, in this example there was a mismatch between strategic and operating plans. The reason for this was lack of understanding at the operating level of what the strategic plan now required of the operating system. No effort had been made to translate strategic imperatives into explicit priorities for the operating system. Without these, traditional functional priorities prevailed.

In most organizations, there is seldom consensus on what is really important. This has disastrous consequences for strategy implementation. When there is no agreement on what is most important and on where the organization should focus resources, there is no foundation for successful execution of any plan.

Once the demands of the strategic plan on the operating system are identified, the OPG considers the *gap* between the operating system's current performance and the level required to satisfy each major demand. The area where the gap is greatest becomes the highest priority for improving operating system perform-ance, the next greatest gap is the second priority and so on. When these priorities are made explicit and communicated widely, all managers understand and can focus their efforts on the most important areas for performance improvement.

Furthermore, these priorities for improving an operating system's performance can then be applied as a set of screening criteria to the already developed list of high-leverage targets. The result is a prioritized set of objectives for the operating plan.

Using priorities to link operating to strategic plans has three important bene-fits. One, it identifies where management should focus its resources to ensure successful execution of the business strategy. Two, it provides the means for ensuring that all members of management throughout the organization are in agreement about this focus. Three, it ensures tight alignment between the strate-gic business plan and the operating plans on which its successful execution depends.

Operating System Capabilities

There is a third factor on which an OPG must reach consensus in order to form a useful mental model for selecting the 3–5 foundation strategies for an operating plan. This is an assessment of the operating system's capabilities to perform in ways required of it by the strategic plan. Such an assessment is typically expressed as strengths and weaknesses … a topic discussed earlier in this Chapter.

When in formulating a strategic plan a PG assesses an SBU's capabilities, it considers the entire organization relevant to the SBU. When there are many peo-ple working in more than a single facility, there is typically more than one operat-ing system involved. Often, the performance capabilities of operating systems vary, even when all support the same SBU. Any PG's assessment would be more broad-brush and less focused and accurate than one made by an OPG for a single oper-ating system. Thus assessments of operating system capabilities should be regarded as more valid and given more weight than assessments of SBU capabilities.

An assessment's validity depends on contextual relevance, comprehensiveness and objectivity. In my earlier discussion of assessing SBUs' capabilities, I made the point that any SBU characteristic is a true strength or weakness only relative to competitors' characteristics and in light of intended strategic business objec-tives. These form the *context* for the assessment. In evaluating operating system capabilities, the context is the strategic business plan and its objectives. A partic-ular characteristic of an operating system should be deemed a strength if it enhances the probability of successful strategic plan execution, and a weakness if it represents a barrier or obstacle.

Earlier in my discussion of high-leverage targets, I noted that a comprehensive description of an operating system and its analysis are necessary prerequisites to identifying these targets. Such a description and analysis also ensures that the system capability assessment is comprehensive. Before it makes this assessment, an OPG will already be aware of and have considered all principal elements of the operating system.

Ensuring that the capability assessment is objective means minimizing any tendencies towards wishful thinking or pessimism. It is natural for members of any organization to be proud of certain characteristics, and to feel frustrated about others. Care should be taken, however, in equating strength with pride and weakness with frustration. This trap can be avoided in the OPG by explicitly testing whether a characteristic is truly a strength or weakness. This can be done by comparisons with known competitors and by referring to the context.

Greater objectivity can also be encouraged by systematic examination of past efforts to improve the operating system's performance. Each of several past improvement efforts should be reviewed as to the success or failure of results achieved. Then explanations for each of the outcomes should be sought, and any patterns of behavior identified. Such revisiting of the past helps an OPG to learn new, more objective lessons from the organization's experience and to dispel myths based on incomplete or distorted information.

Another means for improving objectivity is inviting each member of the OPG (or a broadly representative group of managers and supervisors within the operating system) to respond to a confidential questionnaire dealing with perceptions of how well or poorly various elements of the system are working. Analysis of the responses will reveal any widely perceived problem areas along with other aspects of the system that people believe to be functioning well. These data can be used as an additional input into the analysis of strengths and weaknesses (8).

Choosing Foundation Strategies and Developing an Operating Plan's Superstructure

Once an OPG agrees on operating system priorities, a prioritized list of high-leverage targets and an assessment of the system's capabilities, it has formed a mental model for choosing 3–5 foundation strategies for the operating plan. The OPG applies this model to screen the 33 generic strategy options (Appendix C) and translates its choices into no more than 5 strategy statements tailored to fit its operating system. This process is no different from that described earlier for the

SBU's strategic business plan. Similarly, for each strategy, an Action Planning Group (APG) is formed and asked to formulate a proposed action plan.

The superstructure for an operating plan contains the same elements as that for an SBU's strategic plan. There is an integrated action program outlining tasks, deliverables, timetables, resources and accountabilities. There is a process for measuring and monitoring accomplishments and progress in executing the operating plan. There are assumptions about future events outside management's control that are key to successful plan execution. There is a list of the major qualitative changes to the operating system expected to result from successful plan execution. There is an analysis of risk of implementation failure. There is a plan for communicating the operating plan and its subsequent implementation achievements and progress to people within and perhaps outside the operating system.

Each of these elements is like its counterpart in the strategic plan, except that its focus is on the operating system rather than on the SBU. The process for formulating each element is the same as that described in the earlier section on strategic plans, and for the same reasons. By forming an OPG with relevant, knowledgeable people and applying the process already described, two simultaneous outcomes are likely. A high quality plan will be formulated to change the way an operating system works so that it effectively supports execution of the strategic plan. Concurrently, the managers accountable for plan execution understand the operating plan thoroughly and are committed to carrying it out successfully.

7. A Process for Measuring Performance, Monitoring Implementation Progress, and Updating Strategic and Operating Plans

However well conceived, no strategic or operating plan can be regarded as valid for more than several months. Circumstances change in unanticipated ways, both externally and internally. Unexpected problems and obstacles arise to undermine plan execution. No one can forecast the future accurately. Also, no strategic or operating plan, however brilliant, has any worth until it is implemented. What then, can management do to ensure plan implementation no matter what unexpected problems arise?

The answer lies in another key element of SONG. Management must institute and continuously apply a process designed to achieve three aims concurrently. This process enables management to measure its performance in executing both the SBU's strategic plan and the supporting operating systems' operating plans. With this process management can monitor progress and identify accomplishments as plans are implemented. The process also enables management to modify plans whenever circumstances change and whenever unanticipated problems arise. *This process is equal in importance to that for formulating high-quality strategic and operating plans.*

In the prior Sections 5 and 6, I noted that an important element of strategic and operating plans' superstructure is a process designed to measure and monitor implementation progress. In this section, I discuss what such a process should look like, and what it takes to gain the benefits this process can provide.

Key Elements of the Process

Five design criteria define effective processes for measuring and monitoring plan implementation and for continuously updating the plans themselves.

1. Are assignments of *accountability* for plan execution explicit?
   There should be clearly designated individuals assigned accountability for each distinct strategy, program, project, and for each component task.

2. Does each program, project and component task have clearly established *dates for starting and completing* the work?
   When there are interim milestones for projects or tasks of long duration, these too should have assigned completion dates.

3. Are *outputs or deliverables* clearly defined for each program, project, and task?
   Typical deliverables are decisions, consensus, designs, plans, reports, recommendations, agreements, contracts, evaluations, etc.

4. Is there a *tailored package of measures* for each strategy, program and project?
   Measures must not be generic, but instead fitted to the circumstances and plan, and there must be several different kinds of measures.

5. Are there sufficiently frequent regularly scheduled performance reviews involving all key players?
   These are opportunities for everyone accountable to discuss and take stock of progress, and to make any necessary adjustments to plans.

All these questions should be discussed and answered by PGs and OPGs as they formulate strategic and operating plans. Conclusions reached are documented in the plans themselves. I elaborate further on Criteria 4 and 5 below.

A Tailored Measurement Package

Performance measurement is daunting. In essence, the problem is how to measure the impact of certain investments and application of resources on the performance of complex systems ... SBUs in the case of strategic plans, and operating systems in the case of operating plans.

This problem is daunting for several reasons. One is that nobody today knows how to measure with any kind of precision, the impact of a particular change on a system. The many forces that interact within any system are simply too complicated and subtle to identify and isolate cause-effect relationships unarguably. Another reason is that often, the ultimate arbiter of performance (whether the system has actually achieved management's objectives) is *outside* the organizational system ... namely the customer, regulator, funder, investor, supplier, or other stake-holder. Another reason is that almost every traditional measure is seriously flawed. A measure may in fact encompass more than it purports to measure (i.e. every attempt to measure individual performance also measures the performance of the system in which that person works). Or the measure itself may stimulate unwanted behavior ("What you measure is what you get!"). Yet another reason is that executives' expectation and use of measurement are often unrealistic and destructive (i.e. use of "league tables" comprised of inappropriate indicators to compare performance among departments, offices or plants) (9), (10).

Despite these difficulties with measurement, measures must be defined because they are crucial for ensuring successful plan execution. There are four ways by which management can finesse the inherent difficulties noted above and develop measures useful for tracking and monitoring plan implementation. It can approach the problem with an awareness and sensitivity to the problems and limitations already noted. It can focus on measuring *improvement* rather than absolute position (improvement indicated by a trend using a flawed measure is a more reliable finding than any point position on that trend). It can also take a trial-and-error approach to developing measures. This means recognizing from the outset that the set of measures applied ultimately might differ somewhat from the measures adopted initially. Each measure must be tested over time, reviewed and possibly modified before concluding that it is truly valid and useful. Sometimes a measure will prove meaningless or impractical. In such instances, it should be discarded from the measurement package.

Most important, management can use many different measures rather than relying on a few. Some measures should reflect the entire system's performance. Others should focus on particular elements of that system. These can be identified by looking at the action plans for outcomes that would indicate successful execution of strategies, both individually and collectively. A PG or OPG, after reviewing a completed action program, asks, "If we are successful in completing this work, where will we find evidence of progress or improvement?" "If customers will be more satisfied, how and in what dimensions?" "If new market offerings are required, what are the criteria for success?" "If there will be more efficient use of resources, how and where will this be evident?" Answers to these questions are clues to what should be measured and how.

The combination of these targeted measures with broader measures of overall system performance will result in a *tailored measurement package* aligned with the strategic or operating plan. For each measure, management then establishes a performance base line (actual performance during a representative prior period) and later develops a trend chart by applying the measure over a subsequent time period. By reviewing these trends, individually and collectively, management can, with some confidence, assess implementation progress.

A major issue in organizational performance measures is the potential for incongruence that can adversely impact waste, lack of focus and overall system effectiveness. In any organization, measuring performance goes on simultaneously at three distinct levels.

At the top *business* level, only two kinds of measures are key for the strategic plan. These focus on the market (changes in market share, penetration, growth, etc.) and financial performance (changes in profits or surplus, cash flow, returns, assets, margins, earnings, fund balance, etc.).

At the *operating systems* level, there are three kinds of measures that are key for each operating plan. These are measures of customer satisfaction, productivity and flexibility (the system's ability to change its capacity and to change its market offerings).

At the lowest level in an organization, closest to day-to-day operations, are the *functional departments*. Here there are four kinds of measures that are applied continuously. These are quality of each department's output, its ability to meet delivery commitments consistently, the time taken to process the work through the department, and the waste incurred as work is done in the department (11).

In effectively performing organizations, performance measures at all three levels are in alignment and congruent. This means that top-level business measures relating to markets and finances are translated at the operating system level into measures of customer satisfaction, flexibility and productivity, and these in turn, are translated at the department level into measures of quality, delivery, process time and waste. All measures are internally consistent and support the execution of the business strategy.

Unfortunately, such alignment is rare. Once established, measures, like old soldiers, never die ... even when they are no longer relevant. They don't even fade away. Typically, at the department level ... and this is most crucial because this is the level at which work actually gets done ... organization members are confronted with many different measures. Some are irrelevant to the current business strategy (they may once have been relevant to an earlier strategy). Others encourage focus on activities that actually conflict with current plans, potentially undermining strategy execution (such was the case in the kitchen electrical products case cited in Section 6). Some measures may actually be relevant to work required to execute current strategies.

Measures have a strong influence on what people actually do in organizations. Their influence is perhaps strongest at the departmental level. When departmental managers, supervisors and workers confront a wide array of measures, many of which may have been used for a long time, how are they to know which of these are to be taken seriously? When there is no prioritization, individual interpretation rules. If measures are not internally consistent, it may be impossible to satisfy their collective demands. Typically, the result is lack of focus, squandered resources, and failure to execute plans. This is why performance measures at all three organizational levels must be aligned with one another, all supporting the strategic business plan.

Scheduled Performance Reviews

The heart of any effective monitoring process is regular periodic reviews of progress and accomplishments in implementing plans. These reviews should occur at least quarterly in the early stages of plan execution. Later on, they might be scheduled less frequently.

Each performance review should involve every person assigned accountability for a strategy, program, project and task. All should participate together because such review sessions are opportunities for sharing vital information about strategy execution, for learning from implementation experience, and for applying conclusions from that learning to updating action programs. Modifications to plans are crucial for ensuring that they remain on course and on target, whatever unanticipated problems and changes in the external and internal environment occur.

These reviews also provide opportunities for interaction between an organization's leadership and those who carry out the work required to achieve strategic and tactical objectives. By appearing at review sessions, senior executives can report on business progress, provide other "big picture" information, remind participants of the rationale underlying the strategy and provide general inspiration. As they listen to others' reports and discussion, they also learn about some of the difficulties and unanticipated problems of plan implementation. Such exposure to the realities of what it takes to change the way organizations work can help improve the quality of future objective setting and future plans.

An effective monitoring review session may require at least a half-day meeting, and more often takes the better part of a full day. Here is a typical agenda.

1. Introduction: purpose, objectives and meeting agenda

2. Some words from the organization's leader(s)

3. Review of implementation progress for each strategy, program or project
    A. Overview of accomplishments for entire strategy to date
    B. Report on each component task
        a. Progress made and specific accomplishments
        b. Unanticipated problems encountered & actions taken
        c. What has been learned?
        d. Any recommended changes to plan

4. Review of measures and results
    A. What conclusions can be drawn, individually & collectively?
    B. What changes should be made to the measurement package?

5. Review of key assumptions, expected changes and risk analysis
    A. Are assumptions still valid? If not, what are the implications?
    B. Any evidence of expected changes? If not, implications?
    C. To what extent is risk analysis still valid? Implications?

6. What has been learned from today's review?

7. In light of 6, what changes (if any) should be made to the plan?

8. What should be communicated, to whom, and how?

9. Closing remarks; schedule next review session

Systematically conducted group reviews of implementation progress yield at least five important benefits. One, information is generated and shared that enables adjustments to plans so that they remain valid, no matter what happens after they are initially formulated. Two, learning occurs that improves coordination and actions among teams working on related tasks. Three, all participants gain renewed enthusiasm and commitment to successful plan execution once they learn that more progress is being made than they might have expected initially. Four, organization leaders who participate learn about the realities of achieving organizational change. Five, information is generated that enables broader communication within the organization about implementation progress (see Section 11).

Existing Organizational Systems: Some Introductory Comments

Unlike the seven elements of SONG already discussed, the remaining four elements do not need to be established. They already exist in every organization. They have long histories and traditions. Because they are deeply rooted, they are important parts of an organization's culture and exert a powerful influence on the way organizations and their people behave. These existing organizational systems are: (1) budgets and financial controls; (2) rewards and compensation; (3) management information; and (4) communications.

All these systems are highly relevant to SONGs because they are integral to how organizations work. Depending on their design, they can either impede or facilitate changes crucial to strategy execution. The issue here is not how to create these systems. Rather, it is how to align these systems with current strategic and operating plans so that they do not conflict with and undermine them, but instead support the achievement of strategic objectives.

Ensuring alignment means explicit reviews of each of these four systems whenever there are changes in strategic plans, and making whatever adjustments are required to maximize congruency. The problem in doing this is that these systems are organization-wide, complex and laden with tradition. Making any adjustment is often a daunting task. Making periodic adjustments is even more disruptive and difficult. There are many vested interests and powerful forces for maintaining the status quo. Also, the complexity and scope of these systems present high risks of unintended consequences when any changes are made.

Yet, to ignore the issue of alignment is perilous. Each of these systems can seriously undermine the successful execution of strategic and operating plans. If behavior demanded by a plan of an organization and its people is in direct conflict with behavior encouraged by an existing organizational system, the latter will always prevail. Deeply rooted systems with their historic cultural momentum are far more powerful than any new, relatively short-lived strategy.

In the rest of this chapter, I discuss each of these existing organizational systems. The context for this examination is how to design a SONG that has maximum power and effectiveness.

8. Strategy-Driven Budgets and Financial Controls

Budgets and financial controls have been applied by organizations long before strategic planning. Even today for many organizations, budgeting is the only form of planning or guidance and control in use. Of the four existing organizational systems, budgets and financial control is the one with the longest tradition and the one most deeply rooted and powerful. Consequently, it is the existing system with the greatest potential for undermining successful plan execution.

Consider the basic characteristics of any budget and financial control system. Its primary purpose is to enable management to guide and control an organization's *operations*. This means that it is *internally* and *departmentally* focused and mostly *short term* in outlook (a capital budget may have a longer-term horizon than an expense budget, but in practice, it is the next year that counts most). Typically, a forecasted budget for the following year is prepared initially by departments or functions, then aggregated, and reviewed at operating and business levels. It may then be revised by departments or functions before final approval. Budget categories are well established and standardized. They vary little from one business to another, even among the profit, not-for-profit and government sectors. Financial controls are derived from key budget categories and are established to ensure conformance of actual to forecasted expenditures. The entire system is intended to ensure responsible *fiscal* behavior within the organization and successful *financial* outcomes.

Contrast the above characteristics with those of SONG. Its primary purpose is to enable management to guide and control the formulation and execution of an *organization's strategy*. This means that it is focused first externally and then internally. Its outlook is long- and intermediate-term. Almost all work in SONG is done at both business and operating system levels. Departments and functions are involved only as elements of these two systems. The only major departmental task is to align departmental performance measures with those of the operating and business systems (see Section 7). SONGs are intended to ensure successful *business* and *organizational* outcomes.

Clearly there are fundamental differences between SONG systems and budget and financial control systems. One encourages broad, outward-looking, systemic thinking with a far-forward perspective. The other encourages a narrow, detail-oriented, inward-looking thinking with one eye on the near-term and the other on the rear-view mirror.

Collision occurs between these two systems when there is no provision in the budget for resources required to execute strategic and operating plans. This can happen when people at departmental level in the course of preparing their budget forecast, fail to understand (or believe) what and how their department must contribute to successful plan implementation. Typically, departments develop budget forecasts by extrapolating past years' actual expenditures and then seasoning these with contingency provisions. Unless departments fully understand what will be required of them by current strategic and operating plans, their budget forecasts will have little relation to intended strategies. When it comes time to execute the strategy and it is discovered that there is no money in the budget for key requirements, there is a high probability that the budget will prevail and implementation will stall.

How then can such a problem be avoided? How can these two disparate systems be better aligned? The answer lies in taking an approach to budget development that is different from traditional methods. This new approach is strategy-driven. The key element of strategic and operating plans on which to focus is action programs.

Departments and functions develop strategy-driven budgets in the following way:

1. Each department or function first determines the minimum base line budget it requires merely to continue its existence. This "readiness" level provides a minimum level of basic capabilities for response to any general strategic demands. It does not provide for the specific demands of particular strategic and operating plans (i.e. a marketing department will need a basic, minimum-level market research capability to support any marketing strategy, whatever its particular demands might be).

2. Each action program for both strategic and operating plans is analyzed, task by task, to identify any work required of the department. If the department is called upon to make a contribution, any associated expense is noted by traditional budget category. If any revenues might accrue to the department, these too are noted.

3. For each strategy and its supporting action plan, expenses required are totaled and are offset by any revenues. The resulting net expense (by line-item) is then layered above the "readiness" base-line budget.

Formulating a strategy-driven budget requires first that the budget be developed *after* the development of strategic and operating plans. All too often in many organizations, the budget cycle is independent of the planning cycle. By taking the approach described above, the resulting budget is fully aligned with strategic and operating plans. Any potential conflict will have been eliminated. By ensuring that departmental measures are congruent with measures used to track implementation progress for strategic and operating plans (see Section 6), financial controls will also be aligned with the business strategy. Following the principle, "What you measure is what you get", departmental activities will be focused on what is important for strategy implementation.

Ensuring that budgets and financial controls are strategy-driven harnesses all day-to-day work done in an organization directly to its strategic and operating plans. This greatly enhances the probability of successful plan execution.

9. Strategy-Driven Rewards and Compensation

Reward and compensation systems generally have two major elements. One is the way people are paid for their work. This includes how pay packages are structured (fixed and variable components, and the nature of these components), pay levels, their inter-relationships, increases in pay, and how all this is determined. The other element is the basis for changes in status and advancement within the organization.

Existing compensation and reward systems, especially for executives and managers, have the same potential for undermining successful strategy implementation as do budgets and financial controls. Powerful messages are sent by criteria for rewards and compensation together with the level of rewards and compensation. These messages signal executives and managers what is truly valued in the organization and what they should consider really important in performing their daily tasks.

For example, at middle and lower levels of management, compensation may be predominantly fixed with little, if any opportunity for additional variable bonus based on actual performance. Here there is a clear message that actual performance doesn't count for much. It's position and perhaps longevity that really matter. In such instances, the compensation and reward system contributes little to a SONG. It is either a neutral or demotivating force for effective strategy formulation and execution. So long as the status quo is maintained, rewards and compensation are essentially unaffected.

By contrast, if the variable bonus portion of executive compensation is substantial, how that bonus is determined becomes significant. In many instances (especially in the profit sector), executive bonuses depend primarily on the organization's annual financial performance. Typically, measures vary little year-to-year, and include profitability, various return ratios and changes in share value. Compensation packages may also include company stock and options to purchase shares.

In the context of SONG, this approach to compensation is problematic. The message conveyed is that short-term improvement in the company's financial performance is what really matters. It is unlikely that any executive would feel encouraged to pursue any strategy requiring substantial near-term investment (which would reduce this year's bonus) in order to achieve an improved market position with possible long-term benefits. Rather, the motivation would be to consider strategies with positive near term financial impacts.

As for non-financial rewards, these too send signals of what behavior is truly valued in the organization and what behavior is discouraged. Who gets promoted to what jobs and why? Who is penalized by being moved to less desirable jobs and why? What happens to risk-takers? How executives and managers interpret these signals influences their choice of strategic options and their commitment to executing certain strategies.

Like budget and financial control systems, compensation and reward systems often have long histories and are laden with tradition. They are integral with organizational cultures. Any attempts to change these systems encounter powerful resistance from vested interests in maintaining the status quo. Because these systems are complex and subtle in the way they impact people's behavior, there is also serious risk that any changes will produce unanticipated unwanted consequences.

Yet, to ensure a powerful SONG, compensation and reward systems must be aligned with strategic and operating plans (12). To achieve this requires first that everyone in the organization, from executives to workers, have some variable component to their pay. The variable portion of the pay package should depend on the degree to which that job can influence strategic and operating plan formulation and execution. The greater the opportunity to influence, the greater should be the variable component of pay. Thus for example, 50–65% of senior executives' pay could be variable, while workers' pay could contain a variable component, if any, of only 5–10%. The fixed component of pay should be set at (or slightly below) levels determined by considering equity and competitiveness in relation to comparable job rates in the community.

The next step in achieving strategy-driven compensation is to establish criteria for determining the variable component amount actually paid, and the frequency of payment. These criteria should all be derived from how well strategic and operating plans are formulated and successfully executed. Special care must be taken to assess the actual opportunity for influence or leverage each job has on planning and implementation.

For example, each senior executive and manager might negotiate annually with his/her boss, a set of criteria developed from the current strategic or operating plan. Suppose there are four key strategic plan objectives: (1) improve market share by 10% within three years; (2) bring two new products to market within 42 months; (3) improve customer satisfaction by 4 percentage points within two years; and (4) improve return on investment by 3 percentage points within three years. For each objective, the SBU head agrees on an interim goal for the next year. S/he also agrees on a formula that would result in full bonus credit if 100% of the interim goal were achieved, less if there was a shortfall and more if it were exceeded. There is also agreement on how to weight each of these four criteria. The actual total money available for bonuses would depend on year-end profits. The portion of the total available for bonuses at each job level is a matter of policy.

Similar negotiations would take place between senior functional and middle-level department managers. In each instance only those strategic and tactical objectives relevant to the individual's area of responsibility would be considered. Department managers would more likely focus on operating plan rather than strategic objectives.

This approach can also be extended to lower organizational levels. Each supervisor and individual contributor would negotiate with her/his boss a set of personal objectives derived from the operating plan. A weighting and formula for determining the bonus would be agreed in the same way described above.

In effect, I am advocating an approach to compensation based on the concept of management-by-objectives (MBO). My approach differs from traditional MBO in two critical areas. One, all objectives established are derived from either the current strategic or operating plan. At higher organizational levels, these are the plan objectives themselves. At lower levels, the objectives may derive from those particular tasks in the action program relevant to the individual. The other difference is that all objectives are established by negotiation and agreement between the individual and his/her boss.

Any "merit" increases to the fixed portion of pay should be based on whether the individual has met, exceeded or slipped commitments made in relation to executing strategic or operating plans and/or personal MBOs. These increases should signal that superior, average and disappointing performers are rewarded very differently. For example, a superior performer would receive an annual increase of at least 15% in contrast to 7% or less for an average performer. Consideration should also be given to increasing the frequency of awards to superior performers (2–3 times annually rather than once).

Personal contributions to successful plan implementation should also determine any awards of company stock and stock options. The amount would be based both on criteria similar to those outlined above and on the individual's leverage in formulating and executing strategy.

As for non-monetary rewards, any changes and advancement of status within the organization should also be based on effectiveness in contributing to strategy formulation and its successful execution. Consistent, clear signals should be sent to everyone in the organization that performance and achievement in the context of formulating and executing plans are what really matter.

The overall objective in achieving tight alignment of an organization's reward and compensation system with its SONG is to establish and sustain a culture that values effective planning and execution as collaborative, group activities, and making and meeting commitments as individual ones. Such a culture will establish SONG as the core system for managing the business and the organization.

10. Strategy-Driven Management Information

An organization's management information system (MIS) is another existing system that has usually developed independently of strategic planning. It consists of an aggregation of measures, indices, standards, controls, quantitative and qualitative data and reports that were established and accreted over time. When any MIS is designed initially, its form is determined by management's stated requirements at that time. Often additions to the system are introduced to meet specific timely needs for information by various levels of management and by various functions and departments. Seldom are elements discontinued. Typically, most data analysis and reporting is computerized, and some of the data input may be automated.

The characteristics of MIS in most organizations resembles that of departmental performance measures described in Section 6. Managers are confronted with an overwhelming amount of information. Some is provided in a timely fashion. Others come too late to be useful. Some is useless or irrelevant. Others may have some interest but may divert attention from what is truly important. Some may actually help managers make intelligent choices in formulating strategy and improve their effectiveness in implementing plans.

Information is a critical tool for managing any business or organization. But the information must be useful and easy to use. This means that information provided to executives and managers must be focused ... relevant to their decision-making needs ... and timely. It must be provided in formats that promote ready and accurate understanding and easy application.

Strategy is what makes facts relevant or irrelevant. Strategy also makes relevant facts significant or insignificant. MIS must be strategy-driven. This means that the design of an MIS should be based on what is required to formulate high quality strategic business plans and supporting operating plans. An MIS must provide PG and OPG members with information they need (both external and internal to the organization) to make the analyses and strategic and tactical choices described in Sections 5 and 6. An MIS must also provide the information needed to execute strategic and operating plans successfully (Section 7).

MIS designers need to understand first how management defines the organization's business(es), SBU(s) and operating systems. They also need to understand any changes. These definitions determine how databases and reports are structured. Then MIS designers need to understand the kinds of data, information and reports needed to identify industry and market characteristics and trends, competitors' and funders' characteristics and strategies, and to assess competitive position and customer satisfaction. They need to understand what is needed to assess the performance of operating systems. They also need to understand what is needed to track the organization's performance as strategic and operating plans are implemented.

In addition, particular strategies may make special demands on MIS for support.

> For example, recall in Chapter 3 the regional insurance company marketing its offerings through funeral homes. MIS was a key element of this firm's new strategy of offering funeral homes a sophisticated, integrated package of services designed to help them enter and succeed in the pre-need business. All components of this package (business planning, lead management tools, selection and training of pre-need counselors, and pre-need insurance) depended on new kinds of information and on support from sophisticated information and computer technology.

An MIS should be designed to maximize the organization's learning from its experience of working with SONG year-to-year. With MIS support, management can improve its skills in using SONG. As it does so, the full power potential of SONG is realized, enabling management and the organization to achieve true success.

Clearly, an MIS is a critical ingredient for effective SONGs and for successful plan formulation and execution. The best way to achieve and maintain alignment of MIS with strategic and operating plans is to ensure that key MIS managers are actively involved as members of PGs and OPGs.

11. Communications

Every organization has an existing formal communications system that, like departmental measures and MIS, has developed over time, independent of strategic planning and execution. Unlike other organizational systems however, formal communications systems are seldom designed intentionally. Instead, they evolve organically. Their nature reflects management styles of past and current leadership. A communications system is an integral element of an organization's culture, and is best viewed as its lubricant.

Formal communications systems are networks which provide means for conveying messages and information from sources to targets, and for conducting dialogues and interactions among people, wherever they may actually be located. Formal communications systems operate primarily within organizations, but also extend outward to include external stakeholders ... suppliers, funders, shareholders, regulators, legislators, the media and the community in general. Organizational communications systems enable messages and information to flow top->down, bottom->up and laterally within the organizational structure, and also inside->out and outside->in.

Every organization also has an informal communications system generally known as "the grapevine" which co-exists with and augments the formal system. Grapevines are ubiquitous and anarchic. They are like the internet, except that everyone has access. Grapevines tend to work far more rapidly and efficiently than formal communications systems, but messages and information carried may be less reliable because of vulnerability to unfounded rumor. As grapevines are uncontrollable, I am confining the following discussion to formal communications systems. It is important, however, to be aware of grapevines and their power, and to use them to augment the formal system whenever possible.

A useful way to think about formal communications systems is to view them as organizational lubricants. The easier it is for messages and information to flow in every direction, and the greater the volume of messages and information that flow, the more effectively will the organization function. Communications systems lubricate SONGs in the same way.

Any existing communications system can be tailored to ensure that SONG is well lubricated. Here are the key characteristics of a tailored communications system.

1. There are established links between the organization and key sources of external information: customers, suppliers, funders, distribution channels, industry experts (including trade publications and business analysts), government legislators and regulators. By providing *continuous* information about

the external environment (industry and market trends, customer needs and satisfaction, competitors' strategies and characteristics) these links support the development of appropriate Business Definitions, the CEO's Provisional Strategic Guidelines, the Base Future Scenario and the SBU's Strategic Business Plan.

2. There are mechanisms for documenting, disseminating, and getting feedback questions and responses from within the organization on key elements of SONG: Business Definition; Definitions of Business and Operating Units; the CEO's Provisional Strategic Guidelines; Base Future Scenario; Strategic Business Plans; Operating Plans; Measuring and Monitoring Process; and an annual SONG calendar (Chapter 7).

3. There are mechanisms for launching implementation of strategic and operating plans. These enable management to announce and describe plans to everyone impacted (within and outside the organization), and enable the latter to raise questions and get answers.

4. There are mechanisms for keeping everyone concerned (both within and outside the organization) informed periodically about implementation progress and accomplishments, for raising questions and answering them, and for encouraging the contribution of ideas to enhance plan execution.

In the context of SONG, the purpose of a communications system is twofold. It should enhance the quality of strategic and operating plans by providing continuously, current, comprehensive, strategically relevant information about the organization and its external environment. The system should also maximize people's understanding and involvement, primarily within but also outside the organization, so that everyone concerned will identify with the objectives of strategic and operating plans, and thus contribute to their successful execution.

Communications systems that provide excellent support to SONGs employ a wide range of media and techniques. Strategic and operating plans are launched by senior executives and managers conducting a series of meetings, each with a group of 20–60 employees. There is an initial presentation outlining plan highlights and rationale, using visual aids that may include a videotaped message from the CEO. A specially prepared summary of the plan in a printed document is then distributed. Small groups of 5–7 organization members are formed to discuss the plan and formulate questions. Small groups provide an environment more conducive than a large group for open discussion, and also provide anonymity for raising questions. Each meeting concludes with management's responses to the questions raised.

As implementation proceeds, similar (but shorter) meetings are used to keep everyone concerned current about progress and accomplishments. Meeting agendas are driven by outputs from the periodic monitoring sessions described in Section 7. Between these meetings, organization members are kept informed of progress by articles in organizational news organs, special newsletters, mailings to the home and measurement trend charts posted and updated in suitable locations (e.g. outside common eating and rest areas). Specially designed posters can add impact. If the organization has an intranet, this can be a powerful addition to the communications system, especially among management.

All of the above is aimed at answering questions and reducing anxiety that people inevitably have when confronting changes that will impact them (13). As implementation begins, people want to know answers to such questions as, "How is this plan helping our customers?", "What is the plan trying to accomplish, and why?", "How and when do we expect to achieve these objectives?", "What resources will be applied?", "What changes does the plan require?", "How will we know if we're succeeding?", "What must I do differently?" and "What does all this mean to me?"

People outside the organization are kept informed about plans and implementation progress mostly by the written word and videotapes. But in key areas more personalized interactive meetings are appropriate. Also, a web page on the internet can be very effective.

In the profit sector, all this communication of strategically-relevant information may raise concern about the security of the company's plans in a competitive marketplace. It is impossible to share such information broadly and expect secrecy to be preserved. Management must carefully consider the trade-off between the risks of such communications and information sharing, on the one hand, and the benefits of broad understanding, of involvement in and commitment to successful plan execution on the other.

Postscript: Some Thoughts About Organizational Structure

In my discussion of the eleven elements of SONG, I have intentionally not included organization structure. Clearly, structure is an important element of organizational systems. Also, structure has a powerful influence on system effectiveness and how people in that system behave. Yet, I believe that structure should not be considered part of SONG.

SONGs are systems and processes for guiding and controlling the way organizations choose and achieve strategic and tactical objectives. As such, they are dynamic mechanisms for changing the way organizations work. Although this may eventually suggest or require changes in organizational structure, I believe that such changes should be the last element of organizational systems to be changed, not the first.

Changing structure alters relationships and the use of power. This is usually very disruptive and highly traumatic for people in the organization. It can often be demoralizing and anxiety producing. The result is often distraction from work and an undermining of organizational effectiveness. Also, because organizational systems are so complex and subtle in the way they work, any structural change is likely to produce many undesirable unanticipated effects along with those that are intended.

> I was once engaged as a consultant by the CEO of a sizeable manufacturing company. One of the largest firms in the U.S. during World War II, this company's business had since fallen precipitously. Because it failed to keep pace with changing technology in its industry it was unable to provide the market with a product to follow-on its once dominant one. At the start of my assignment, the company had become essentially a large job shop with no sustaining product except the spare parts for its original market offering.
>
> The relatively new CEO was a highly intelligent lawyer with no technical credentials. He was trying desperately to regain some of the firm's past glory. He believed that it was crucial to galvanize his senior management group, all long-term veterans of the organization, who were by now quite cynical and without hope. He was convinced that anxiety was the most powerful motivator. He deliberately created a constant climate of anxiety by changing the organizational structure every 3–4 months. But instead of becoming reinvigorated, the management group grew increasingly preoccupied with the shifts in power and internal conflicts. There was no improvement in the situation. After several unsuccessful attempts to dissuade the CEO from his approach, I resigned.

By integrating and orchestrating its use of the eleven elements discussed in this chapter, management can gain maximum benefit from SONG (Chapter 7). When SONG is working at full power, it changes the way an organization works in directions required to enable regular formulation and successful execution of strategies that are in tune with the leadership's agenda, the realities of the external environment and the organization's capabilities. All this can be done *without* changing organizational structure.

In time, it may become evident that certain structural changes would be desirable. Once people see that processes could work more smoothly and effectively if formal relationships were modified, they are more understanding and supportive of structural change. Any formal changes to organization structure should be timed to coincide with people's readiness to accept and support them.

NOTES TO CHAPTER 6

1 Here are some recently published and classic works on strategic planning.

Aaker, D.A., *Developing Business Strategies*, John Wiley, New York, NY, 1995

Barney, J.B., *Gaining and Sustaining Competitive Advantage*, Addison-Wesley, Reading, MA, 1997

Day, G.S., *Market Driven Strategy*, Free Press, New York, NY, 1990

DeThomas, A.R. & Fredenberger, W.B., *Writing A Convincing Business Plan*, Barron's, New York, NY, 1995

Gould, M., Campbell, A. & Alexander, M., *Corporate-Level Strategy*, John Wiley, New York, NY, 1994

Mintzberg H., *The Rise and Fall of Strategic Planning*, Free Press, New York, NY, 1994

Porter, M.E., *Competitive Strategy*, Free Press, New York, NY, 1980

Steiner, G.A., *Strategic Planning*, Free Press, New York, NY, 1979

2 This approach is discussed at length in Judson, A.S., *Making Strategy Happen*, Blackwell Business, Cambridge, MA, 1996

3 Process skills are discussed in Chapter 8, Judson, A.S., *Changing Behavior in Organizations*, Blackwell Business, Cambridge, MA, 1991

4 I describe several such instruments and tools in *Making Strategy Happen*

5 I discuss action planning at length in *Making Strategy Happen*

6 *Making Strategy Happen* is the only book I know that deals extensively with the content and process for developing operating plans

7 Ibid, Chapter 8

8 Ibid, see OMRA questionnaire, Chapter 9

9 For a particularly dramatic example of the adverse effect of measures, see the article on the Internal Revenue Service and its abusive approach to U.S. citizens, *Newsweek*, October 13,1997.

10 For a more extended discussion of measurement, see *Making Strategy Happen*, Chapter 12

11 For a more extended treatment of the concept of the "performance pyramid" see Cross, K.F. & Lynch, R.L., *Measure Up!*, Blackwell Business, Cambridge MA, 1990. Another excellent work on measures is Kaplan, R.S. & Norton, D.P., *The Balanced Scorecard*, Harvard Business School Press, Boston, MA, 1996

12 For an extended treatment of strategy-driven rewards, see Lawler, E. E., *Strategic Pay*, Jossey-Bass, San Fransisco, CA, 1990, and Schuster, J.R. & Zingheim, P.K., *The New Pay*, Jossey-Bass, San Fransisco, CA, 1996

13 For an extended discussion of the dynamics of change and people's resistance to it, see my book, *Changing Behavior In Organizations*

CHAPTER 7

USING SONG IN A SINGLE BUSINESS ORGANIZATION

SONG adds value to an organization when the eleven elements described in Chapter 6 work together continuously. Once management learns how to integrate and orchestrate its use of these elements, it realizes the full power potential of SONG. This benefit is seldom achieved immediately. Rather, it takes several years for an organization's management to become experienced and skilled in applying SONG as a core system and process for running the business and organization. As it learns how to do this, SONG delivers increasing benefits each year.

SONGs work continuously in conjunction with organizations' planning cycles. The length and frequency of these cycles vary with relevant industry characteristics. If changes in an industry occur relatively slowly, an organization in that industry need not review and modify strategy bi-annually, as would be the case for organizations in more dynamic environments. Companies in such industries as financial services, semiconductors, computers, telecommunications and entertainment would review and revise strategic plans at least every two years, while organizations in such industries as social services, certain kinds of mining, basic chemicals, museums, education, and the performing arts might rethink strategies every four to five years.

In this chapter, I discuss how SONG is initially established and how the eleven elements inter-relate. Then I describe how they work together continuously as a core system and process as management gains experience and skill. Throughout the chapter I assume an annual planning cycle coinciding with the calendar year.

Getting Started

An overview of SONG for a single business organization is outlined in Figure 6. The numbers in each module and in the following text refer to the numbered

123

sections/elements in Chapter 6. Here is a reminder. Although the process may appear in Figure 6 as roughly linear and sequential, it is decidedly not! In earlier chapters, I noted points in the process where potential iteration can occur. At these points, conclusions and decisions made at earlier stages may be questioned and challenged at later stages. This requires reconsideration and possible revision of earlier conclusions and decisions. When this happens, much of the work done subsequently needs to be rethought and possibly modified. Points where such iterations may be triggered are indicated in Figure 6 by double-ended arrows. Possible iterations are also discussed throughout the chapter.

A planning cycle is formally launched by distributing the CEO's Provisional Strategic Guidelines (3). Five tasks are completed prior to this. A key initial task is a first cut at defining the business that the organization intends to be conducting in the near term and on into the future (1). This definition must be forward-looking because the current definition may already be obsolete.

> Remember the regional insurance company selling individuals low denomination policies through funeral homes to cover death expenses. This is how the existing business was defined before management began formulating its strategic plan. It was already aware of the major changes rocking the death industry ... entry and growth of large corporations with chains of funeral homes offering integrated packages of ceremony, caskets/urns, flowers, cemetery plots, etc., plus pre-need financing vehicles to pay for all this. As it began its planning cycle, management defined the business it now wanted to be in ... selling independent funeral directors an integrated package of services designed to help them compete with the corporate chains (see Chapter 3).

How a business is defined determines the parameters of the organization's industry ... what other organizations to consider as competitors, as suppliers and funders, as distributors, as regulators and perhaps as customers. Once these have been identified, the dynamics of that industry can be examined ... growth, markets and market offerings and opportunities, financial operating characteristics, use of technology, bases of competition, and trends in all of these areas. All this establishes the scope for industry and market research and for developing a Base Future Scenario (4). As this takes shape and managers gain greater understanding of the external environment, the initial business definition may be challenged. If so, the definition may be revised either prior to or during the strategic plan formulation process (5).

Figure 6
<u>SONG IN A SINGLE BUSINESS ORGANIZATION</u>

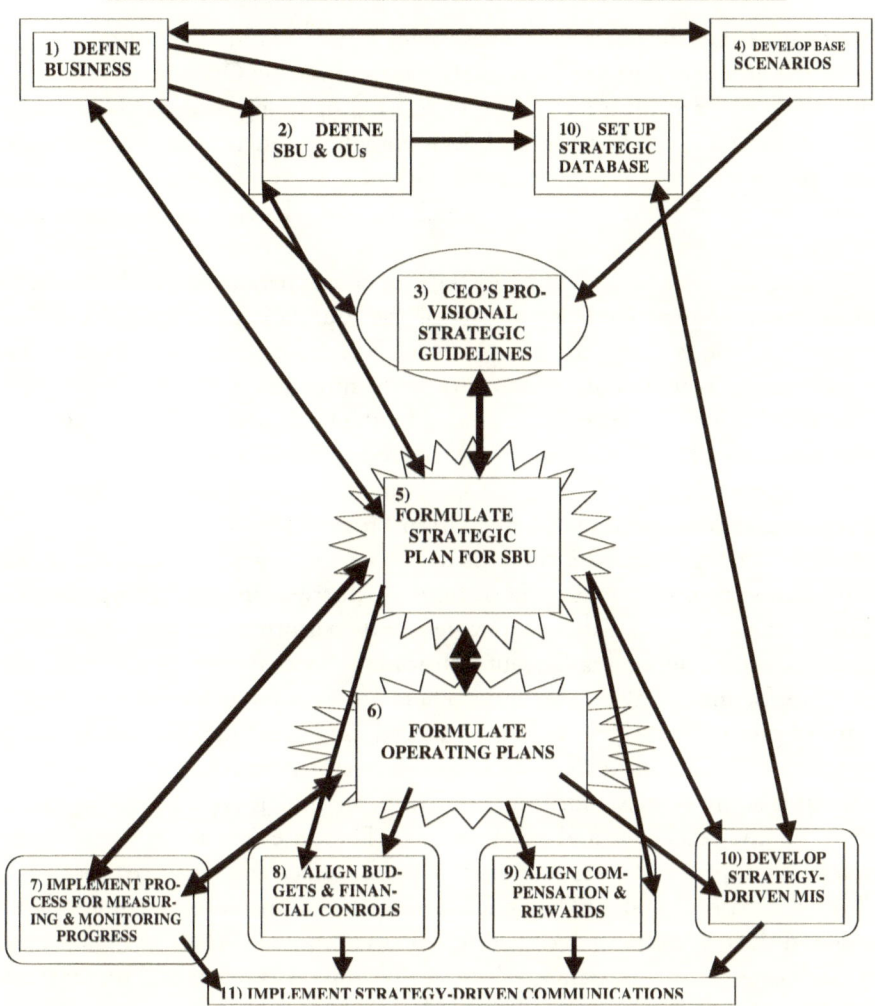

A modest-sized company was providing brokerage and other financial services to more than 1000 financial planning firms throughout the U.S. As it began to formulate its first formal strategic plan, management agreed on an initial definition of its business. Midway through the planning process, as it came to understand more fully the segment of the financial services industry in which it participated, the PG revised the business definition. At the end of the planning process when the PG was conducting its final review of the draft strategic plan, it decided to revise the business definition yet again.

Once it defines the business, management can determine the boundaries and form of the Strategic Business Unit (SBU) and supporting Operating Units (OU) within the entire organization (2). This means designating an executive accountable for conducting the business and deciding which functions and departments should be under her/his direct control. This also means defining the operating system(s) within the organization on which the SBU depends to execute its business strategies.

Defining the business, SBU and OU(s) also sets parameters and criteria for establishing a strategic database as part of the foundation for the MIS (10). A strategic database is designed to support SONG for a particular business. The database should contain data relevant to the formulation and execution of strategy for that business ... everything needed by the CEO and her/his management group (especially the PG and the OPG) to develop Base Future Scenarios (4), the SBU's Strategic Business Plan (5), Operating Plan(s) (6) and the Process for Measuring and Monitoring Implementation Progress (7).

A useful strategic database contains data about industry structure ... the key organizations (competitors, suppliers, funders, distributors, etc.) comprising the industry, their characteristics, strategies and performance over time. Also included are data about markets and customers ... characteristics, classes, segments, needs, and behavior over time. There are data about market offerings ... volume of products and services purchased and used over time. There may also be data about other significant factors in the external environment ... demographics, funding sources, legislation and regulation, technology, and economic factors such as currency exchange and inflation rates. There are data about the SBU: key characteristics, past and current strategies, performance and resources applied.

This database should be dynamic. It should be capable of accommodating changes in the organization and its external environment. When an organization first establishes a strategic database it typically contains some useful material and some irrelevant data. There is also much important data that is not initially included. As management gains experience with its SONG, it learns what data it needs. These are incorporated in the database. Over time, the database grows in size, relevance and usefulness. A key element of a strategy-driven MIS (10), the strategic database helps determine its form and characteristics.

The initial definitions of the business, the SBU and OUs, the Base Future Scenario(s), and the strategic database all provide inputs to the CEO as s/he formulates the Provisional Strategic Guidelines (3). As this statement represents the CEO's *personal* views, s/he determines how much attention and weight is given these inputs. This document initiates the planning cycle and is meant to provide a starting framework for the PG's work. It is crucial that the PG understands, however, that it is free to challenge the CEO's guidelines at any time in the course of the planning process.

The PG is formed by the SBU head, who is usually its most senior-level member. In smaller organizations, the SBU head is the CEO. In larger single-business organizations, the SBU head may be someone other than the CEO. In such instances, the CEO validates the makeup of the PG and may or may not be a member. When the CEO is a participant, challenges to her/his provisional strategic guidelines and their resolution occur in "real time" in the course of the PG's work sessions. When the CEO is not a PG member, any challenges and discussion about revising the strategic guidelines occur in separate scheduled meetings of the PG with the CEO.

Formulating the Plans

Once a CEO validates the PG, it formulates the SBU's Strategic Business Plan (5) using the process described in Chapter 6 Section 5. If the CEO is a member of the PG, the end product is a validated plan. When the CEO is not a participant, the end product is a *proposed* plan, to be reviewed, questioned, and possibly modified by the CEO before it is validated. In the course of the planning process, a PG may question and challenge earlier definitions of the business and of the SBU and OUs. It may also challenge certain aspects of the CEO's Provisional Strategic Guidelines. Such challenges trigger further discussions with the CEO and the top executive group before final resolution is achieved.

The issue of whether or not a SONG requires one or more separate Operating Plans (6) is resolved by the PG during the strategic plan formulation process. In small organizations (fewer than 100 members) operating in a single location, there need not be a separate Operating Plan. The action program in the Strategic Plan suffices. In larger organizations with more than one location, where there are likely to be more than a single operating system, one or more operating plans should be considered.

Four criteria help to determine whether one or more operating plans are appropriate. One is size as measured by number of organization members. Another is number of separate facilities (e.g. offices, production plants, warehouses, distribution centers, wholesale and retail outlets), their locations and size. Another criterion is the uniqueness of each facility's operational capabilities, problems and culture. A fourth criterion is how independent or interdependent are the business processes carried on within each facility, relative to the rest of the organization.

Thus, a facility with more than 25–30 people working in it, located apart from the rest of the organization, with relatively autonomous business processes, will have its own unique history and culture. It will probably be a coherent group with operating capabilities and problems different from those in other parts of the organization. Such a facility is a candidate for its own facility-based operating plan. Alternatively, a similar-sized and located facility with business processes that are highly interdependent with other parts of the organization, may be part of a shared operating plan that addresses an operating system comprised of several facilities (see the discussion of operating systems in Chapters 3 and 6).

Defining operating systems and deciding how many operating plans are appropriate is not a science. These are matters of judgment. Such decisions also depend on trade-offs among (1) the criticality of that facility's contribution to the success of the business strategy, (2) the difficulties in achieving the required changes to that facility's operations, and (3) the investment required to formulate a separate operating plan.

When a Strategic Business Plan is supported by more than a single Operating Plan, management must deal with an additional problem. This is reconciling the potentially conflicting demands for resources that may stem from multiple operating plans. Any OPG working independently will formulate an operating plan focused on addressing the unique problems within the relevant facility or operating system. This plan will require resources both from within the facility or system, and from the rest of the organization. Such a plan cannot be considered automatically validated. Rather, it is a *proposed* plan, to be reviewed, questioned and ultimately validated by the SBU head and CEO.

When there are two or more operating plans, the collective resources requested may exceed the organization's capability to provide these. Also, the aggregate promises of performance improvements may fall short of what is required to achieve the Strategic Business Plan's objectives. In such instances, an additional SONG element is required. The CEO, SBU head and key members of each OPG *together* examine and question each proposed operating plan. Their aim is to assess the soundness of each proposed plan, the credibility of performance improvement promises, and the justification for resource requests. Only after such review can top executives make intelligent decisions about which plans to fund and to what extent, and what plan modifications should be urged. Subsequent to these executive decisions, each OPG reconvenes to revise its proposed operating plan, and resubmit the plan for final executive approval. This process is like the Scrum element for dealing with multi-business organizations, described in Chapters 8 and 9.

In situations where management has determined that one or more operating plans are justified, any OPG can, in the course of formulating its operating plan, raise questions about and challenge certain aspects of the Strategic Business Plan. This occurs when an OPG differs from the PG in assessments of implementation feasibility. OPG members, close to day-to-day operating realities, often see actual problems of changing how an operating system works as more formidable than the view taken by higher-level manager and executive PG members when they formulated the strategic business plan. In larger organizations, PG members tend to be less knowledgeable and more wishful about day-to-day operating realities than are OPG members.

> For example, an American producer of composite cans (containers for frozen juices) wanted to increase its market share in an intensively competitive business. Price was the primary, and responsive delivery service the secondary basis of competition. In the strategic business plan, the PG called for more innovative approaches to reducing costs in the company's many small, highly mechanized can manufacturing plants (each located adjacent to a major customer). The plan specified a strategy based on productivity gains-sharing (see Operating Plan Strategy Option 33 in Appendix C). In developing its operating plan, an OPG in one of the larger plants determined that actual opportunities for employees to offer labor- and cost-saving suggestions were extremely constrained because of the high degree of mechanization. They concluded that the productivity gains-sharing strategy selected by the PG would not work. There was too little latitude for employees to generate the cost savings on which the bonus pool (the basis for cash payouts to employees) depended. Thus there would be insufficient incentive for employees to participate in and contribute to reducing costs. The OPG proposed an alternative strategy to reduce costs and later convinced the SBU head to modify the strategic plan.

It is not unusual for a strategic plan to be called into question by an OPG. When this happens, there is an interaction between the PG and OPG. When the OPG's position is well supported and convincing, the PG must rethink its earlier conclusions and decisions and revise the strategic plan.

Implementing the Plans

Once a Strategic Business Plan (5) and any supporting Operating Plans (6) are formulated, reconciled and validated, implementation begins. High-quality strategic and supporting operating plans include specific plans for Measuring and Monitoring Implementation Progress and Achievements (7). Collectively, these plans describe a comprehensive process for monitoring and motivating successful execution of each strategy in both strategic and operating plans. Further, these plans also establish opportunities for management to learn from its implementation experience, and to apply that learning to make whatever changes are needed to measures and to action plans so that both strategic and operating plans are kept on course and on target.

Well thought out plans for measuring and monitoring plan execution, and for updating plans when necessary create a framework for effective follow-through and successful implementation. However, this framework is useless unless management applies it. The approach described in Chapter 6, Section 7 is straightforward and readily applicable. But in order for it to work, management (especially at senior levels) must act with sustained determination and discipline over the full implementation period (often several years).

The behavioral demands on senior executives are simple but stringent. They must assign individual managers explicit accountability for completing each task in action plans, and for overseeing and coordinating execution of each strategy. They must actually hold each manager accountable for meeting commitments, and consider her/his performance in formal assessments, rewards and compensation. Senior executives must also ensure that the formal, periodic implementation review sessions described in Chapter 6, Section 7 are actually scheduled, and conducted with all the key players present, and that the results are communicated widely. A senior executive should also attend part of each review session, if only to make some introductory remarks. All these actions by top executives must be rigorously consistent, and sustained for whatever time is required to implement the strategic and operating plans.

All this is nothing more than applying basic, sound management principles to following-up execution of previously agreed plans. When senior executives do this, the impact on successful plan execution is profound. Everyone in management and almost everyone else in the organization sees that the organization's leaders are truly serious about achieving the long- and intermediate-term objectives articulated in strategic and operating plans. This has a powerful effect on people's understanding of priorities, and helps to keep the organization focused as strategies are implemented. There is also a strong force motivating people to deliver on promises and meet commitments.

When senior executives sustain their attention on the Process for Measuring and Monitoring Implementation Progress (7), this SONG element becomes fully as important as high quality strategic and operating plans. A consistently well-managed monitoring process can, in fact, make up for any weaknesses or deficiencies in the plans themselves. Organizational learning from systematic, comprehensive group reviews of implementation progress enables management to redirect and strengthen action plans and sometimes even to change strategies.

> A large Canadian fertilizer manufacturer supplies North American farmers with both nitrogen- and potash-based products through whole-sale distributors. Believing that it was conducting two different businesses (nitrogen and potash fertilizers) management had formulated and was executing two separate strategic plans. After 18 months of implementation, management became convinced from learning generated by systematic progress reviews, that similarities in the nitrogen and potash "businesses" far outweighed any differences. Management decided to merge the two "businesses" into a single North American Wholesale Fertilizer SBU with a single strategic plan.

Sadly, I have had mixed experience with senior executives' ability to ensure sustained, disciplined, systematic follow-through on strategy implementation. Initially, every CEO with whom I have worked displayed genuine interest and determination to establish and use SONG as the core process for managing. All participated actively and enthusiastically in formulating strategic plans. Once this work was done, however, the extent of their continued involvement varied. Some CEOs sustained their attention, ensuring that the monitoring process was implemented as planned. They appeared and spoke at review sessions and held managers accountable for their commitments. In these cases, SONG worked well and grew in power.

Other CEOs, however, were unable to sustain attention. After one or two review sessions, they no longer appeared. There was scant evidence that assignments of accountability had any real meaning. Broken promises increased in frequency with no apparent consequences for the managers responsible. Attendance at review sessions became spotty. Planned progress reviews were often rescheduled and intervals between reviews lengthened.

If implementation monitoring is such an important SONG element, and doing the work required is so straightforward, why do so many well intended CEOs fail to ensure that this work is done? The problem here is how to sustain focus over a period of one to three years on something that appears to be somewhat mundane. Many CEOs view follow-through as work far less exciting and appealing than creating strategy. Executing strategy is regarded as work for lower organizational levels. Once implementation is underway, these CEOs lose interest and get distracted by activities perceived as more appealing. They also get derailed by crises. When this happens, a SONG's power wanes and the investment to establish it is wasted.

I believe that CEOs who view implementation follow-up as relatively routine, unexciting drudgery are myopic and wrong. Certainly, executing plans is work necessarily done by those organization members closest to the operational level, whatever department or function is involved. But it is far from mundane to oversee and monitor this work, match actual progress with what was anticipated in the plan, examine unexpected developments and obstacles, analyze this experience to identify what can be learned and apply the lessons learned to modifying the plan. This analytical and creative work demands many of the same skills as required for strategic planning. Top executives who fail to understand this are missing the boat.

Aligning Existing Organizational Systems

Modifying existing organizational systems to bring them more tightly in alignment with current strategies is often a substantial, complex and subtle undertaking. The work involved initially requires extensive research to understand each system's characteristics and how these influence people's current behavior in the organization. Next there is a design phase when various system modifications are developed and considered. Each potential modification is aimed both at eliminating anything that conflicts with or that might undermine successful plan execution, and at enhancing anything that would encourage and reinforce desired behaviors. The potential impact of each possible modification must then be studied, before proposing actual changes for executive approval. Special care must be taken to identify any undesirable side effects and unintended consequences. It may take as long or longer to achieve alignment as it does to implement an operating plan.

Work to align existing organizational systems with current strategy begins in parallel with plan implementation. Misalignment of Budgets and Financial Controls (8), Compensation and Rewards (9) and MIS (10) may not cripple plan execution, but it may present substantial obstacles that slow progress. As alignment improves (this is typically a gradual process), existing organizational systems become increasingly powerful in supporting and reinforcing plan execution.

Efforts to align budgets and controls, rewards and MIS can be developed by PGs and documented as distinct action plans incorporated within the strategic plan. Alternatively, this work can also be positioned as separate programs, assigned to specially designated task teams. In larger organizations where the SBU head is not the CEO, alignment programs should be accountable to the CEO. This is because any changes to existing organizational systems impact the entire organization, not just the SBU.

How SONG Works Once Established

In this chapter I describe the initial establishment of SONG. In organizations where none of the eleven elements already exist, this is a major undertaking requiring substantial investment of resources. These are mostly management's time, but could also include contracted research to develop comprehensive characterizations of the organization and its external environment. After the first complete cycle, less work is required to continue in succeeding cycles. One reason for this is that once research has been completed to describe the organization and its external environment, updating these descriptions in the next one or two cycles is a matter of focusing only on what has changed since the initial research. Comprehensive studies of the organization and its external environment need be done only once every several years, depending on how rapidly the industry is changing.

Another reason why management's efforts decrease as it applies SONG over time is that it become more practiced and skilled in working with SONG elements. With experience, managers can accomplish what is needed is less time.

Timing: A SONG Calendar

Here is how SONG works in a moderate to large size organization conducting a single business during a typical calendar year planning cycle. During the last quarter of the preceding year, four preparatory tasks are completed. The SBU head and her/his direct reports meet to draft an initial definition of the business (1) and to define what parts of the organization are within the SBU's domain. They also determine whether there are any distinct Operating Units, and if so, how many (2).

Also during this period, a special group of managers are selected to develop one or more Base Future Scenarios (4). Depending on the quality of information available in the organization about its external environment, there may be a need during this period to do comprehensive or focused research on the industry, competitors, suppliers, distributors and funders, and on other external factors. Concurrently, another group of managers and professionals headed up by the Director of Information Services is formed to design and begin developing a strategic database (10).

In early January the CEO reviews the outputs of these four tasks, and develops and writes the CEO's Provisional Strategic Guideline Statement (3). This document is distributed to the organization's managers by mid-January, along with a Planning Calendar.

By the end of the third week in January, the CEO and SBU head form a Planning Group (PG) to formulate the Strategic Business Plan (5). The PG works together in four one- to two-day sessions over the next four months to develop the strategic plan. During the 4–5 week intervals between these group sessions, various assigned tasks are completed by designated groups of managers. These are inputs for succeeding PG sessions. Tasks prior to the initial session are additional research on external matters and research aimed at developing a comprehensive characterization of the organization and its operating systems.

Tasks after the first and second sessions are refining the business definition and the mission statement, and developing proposed action plans for each strategy chosen by the PG as the foundation for the strategic plan. Tasks after the third session are integrating the validated action plans into an action program complete with timetables and assignments of accountability, developing quantified projections of performance improvements and resource requirements, and developing a summary of the financial implications of the plan.

The validated Strategic Business Plan document is completed by the end of May. In early June, execution of the Strategic Business Plan is launched with a series of communications meetings (11) within the organization at which the strategic plan (or a summary) is distributed. In larger, more complex organizations, the CEO, SBU head and her/his direct reports meet in early June to determine whether any separate Operating Plans (6) can be justified, and if so, how many.

In organizations requiring operating plans, the SBU head and her/his direct reports define the operating system(s) that each Operating Plan will address. An Operational Planning Group (OPG) is formed to formulate each proposed Operating Plan. Each OPG works together in three one- to two-day sessions over the next three to four months to develop an Operating Plan. During the 4–5 week intervals between these group sessions, various assigned tasks are completed by designated groups of managers. These are inputs for succeeding OPG sessions. A task prior to the initial session is additional research on organizational characteristics. A task after the initial session is developing proposed action plans for each strategy chosen by the OPG as the foundation for the Operating Plan. Tasks after the second session are integrating the validated action plans into an action program complete with timetables and assignments of accountability, and developing more detailed quantified projections of performance improvements and resource requirements along with their financial implications.

By September, the OPG(s) complete their work. If there is only one Operating Plan, the SBU head validates the OPG's proposed plan by the end of September. When there is more than a single Operating Plan, the SBU head, CEO and key members from each OPG meet for at least 1.5 full days by the end of September to assess the soundness of each proposed plan, to determine whether the aggregate performance improvements promised match the requirements of the Strategic Business Plan, and to determine whether the aggregate resources required can be provided by the organization. If there are any substantial gaps in required vs. promised performance, and requested vs. available resources, the SBU head decides which Operating Plans to validate, and which must be modified. When modifications are required, the relevant OPGs reconvene in October and work out the changes in their proposed operating plans. These are resubmitted for validation.

In October and November, work begins to execute each Operating Plan. As with the Strategic Plan, implementation is launched by a series of communications meetings (11) at which copies of plans (or a summary) are distributed.

The first of periodic formal implementation progress monitoring reviews (7) occurs in October for the Strategic Plan, and January or February of the following year for Operating Plans. Such formal reviews occur every 3–4 months thereafter until implementation has been completed.

As it formulates the Strategic Plan, the PG determines the extent to which existing organizational systems are misaligned with the intended strategy. An Alignment Task Group (ATG) is established for each of the organizational systems requiring modification. By late June, these ATGs begin work to research the problems and formulate recommended changes. By early October, the initial set of recommended changes is submitted to the top executive group for review and approval. Implementation of validated changes to Budgets and Financial Controls (9), Compensation and Rewards (9) and MIS (10) begins by early November.

Preparation of next year's budget occurs during the last quarter of the year. This work is based on the action plans in the Strategic Business Plan, and in Operating Plan(s), together with the summaries of the financial impact. Also during this quarter, work is done to review the business definition, the definitions of SBUs and OUs, the Base Future Scenarios and the strategic database as preparation for the start of the next planning cycle in January.

CHAPTER 8

SONG IN MULTI-BUSINESS ORGANIZATIONS: SOME BASIC ISSUES

When an organization develops beyond conducting a single business, the complexities and difficulties of managing escalate exponentially. Two factors drive this increase in complexity and difficulty: the *number* of businesses in the portfolio; and the extent to which they are *unrelated*. Managing such a portfolio strategically requires resolving at least nine issues peculiar to multi-business organizations (MOs).

SONG can enhance the quality of management's choices about: (a) the makeup of the portfolio; (b) resource allocation; and (c) which strengths and capabilities to leverage across the organization. In order for both SBU managers and MO corporate executives to realize the full potential from their use of SONG, it is crucial that they discuss and reach *explicit agreement* about how to resolve the nine issues listed below. Yet I have found that this seldom happens. In most MOs, the resolution of these difficult issues remains unclear, ambiguous and often inconsistent. Corporate management's intentions are left to interpretation within the organization based on how their actual behavior is perceived. As a result, management is often disappointed in the "yield" from its investment in SONG.

These nine issues are difficult to resolve because there are no easy or "right" answers. Resolving them depends on two considerations. One is the nature of the portfolio itself. The other is the MO's leadership's personal philosophy, taste and level of comfort in engaging and dealing with conflict. Only when management agrees on how to resolve these issues and then translates this agreement into a set of resultant "ground rules" for using SONG, is it able to realize fully the enormous potential power of this core process for managing ..

Here are the issues that an MO's corporate management must resolve explicitly:

1. For any specific business, which decisions are made solely by SBU managers, and which are made jointly with MO corporate executives?

2. When making key decisions about managing a specific business, what is the "balance of power" between SBU and MO corporate management?

3. Which decisions are made solely by MO corporate executives? What role (if any) do SBU managers play in these decisions?

4. As an SBU's strategic plan is executed, who "owns" any profits/surplus (or losses/deficits) … the SBU or MO (corporate)?

5. How much latitude does an SBU have to depart from the agreed (and approved) business definition and mission?

6. What role (if any) does an SBU play in acquisitions, mergers and divestitures?

7. As they execute an agreed (and approved) strategy, SBU managers want to make some fundamental changes. What involvement do MO corporate executives have in making such a decision?

8. What is the appropriate focus of *MO* corporate strategy (as distinct from SBU strategy)?

9. As revenues and returns are actually "delivered" by SBUs, what true value is added by MO corporate executives?

All key players in MO management (both corporate and SBU) need to discuss and agree on how they want to answer these tough questions. They will achieve better answers when their debate is based on a solid understanding both of the nature of their portfolio of businesses and of the realities, principles and dilemmas inherent in SONG.

Some SONG Realities

SONG Defined

SONG is a core management process for planning, directing and managing an organization on an ongoing basis. When more than a single business is being conducted, SONG operates at two (and sometimes three) levels: (a) *individual SBUs and OUs* (organization-wide enabling functions; production facilities; retail outlets); and (b) *MO (as a whole or Corporate)*. When there is a large number of distinct businesses in the portfolio (especially when these are diverse), there may be a third *Group* level between SBUs and Corporate.

At the first level (a), managers use SONG to create the future of a discrete business by setting long-term objectives, formulating plans to accomplish these, and then achieving the sustained focus required to realize desired outcomes. At this level, SONG helps answer such questions as:

- What should we be focusing on … in the marketplace? in the organization?
- Which strategy should we pursue, and what is our plan for carrying this out?
- How can we sustain focus for the time needed to execute our plan?
- When and why should we change our objectives? strategy? focus?

At Group (c) or Corporate level (b), managers use SONG to create the future of either a group of businesses or of the entire MO through structuring and managing the *portfolio* of relevant businesses. With SONG, Group and Corporate executives set Corporate/Group objectives, formulate Corporate/Group strategy and meet Corporate/Group objectives and needs while reconciling these with the differentiated objectives, strategies and needs of each SBU in the portfolio. At this level, SONG helps answer such questions as:

- Which businesses should we be conducting, and how should we define each business?
- Which proposed SBU strategies should be supported? redirected? stopped?
- How should financial, human and other Corporate resources be allocated?
- Where in the MO are there potential synergies? How can these be realized? What capabilities should be leveraged and how?
- How can successful execution of each business strategy be assured?
- When and how should the Corporate/Group portfolio be reconfigured?

Spectrum of MO Postures

When considering the objectives, strategies, concerns, agendas and foci of SBUs on the one hand, and those of Groups and the entire MO on the other, clearly there are fundamental differences (MO and Group are more alike than different). Yet, true success of the organization as a whole depends on *effective reconciliation of these differences.* This occurs only when both parties recognize and acknowledge their *interdependence* and work out ways to transform potential conflicts into mutually beneficial win-wins.

Such transformation is greatly facilitated when everyone involved understands clearly where Corporate leadership position themselves along a spectrum of posture possibilities. This spectrum is defined by a range of alternative models (Figure 7). At one extreme of this spectrum is a *holding company* posture. In this model, each SBU has a high degree of autonomy in setting objectives and formulating and executing strategy and plans. The SBU "owns" any profits/surplus and decides on any reinvestment or acquisitions. So long as objectives are met, Corporate's posture with regard to an SBU is *laissez-faire*. A minimally staffed corporate executive is concerned primarily with structuring and reconfiguring the portfolio of businesses, focusing mainly on acquisitions, mergers and divestitures. SONG works mostly at the SBU level. Corporate leaders focus mostly on financial performance. Growth tends to be less organic and more through acquisition.

> An example of the holding company model was Beatrice Foods Corporation. At its peak in the early 1980's, Beatrice consisted of more than 425 distinct SBUs, almost all of which were acquired from independent entrepreneurs. These SBUs were organized into groups (each headed by a Group President). SBUs varied widely in size and industry … from a wide range of food products and services to luggage, garden and plumbing products, to product and interior design services. Corporate and Group executives and staff numbered fewer than 60. Each SBU operated autonomously, with intervention from Group/Corporate only when performance suffered. The prime corporate objective was continuous quarter-to-quarter improvement in financial performance.

At the other end of this MO posture spectrum is the integrated *corporate strategy model.* Here Corporate not only determines the portfolio of businesses, but also takes a highly pro-active role in formulating and executing each SBU's strategies and plans, and in maximizing opportunities for synergy and leverage among SBUs. Control is shared between Corporate and its SBUs, but Corporate "owns"

Figure 7
ALTERNATIVE MO POSTURE MODELS

CHARACTERISTIC	HOLDING CO.	PORTFOLIO	INTEGRATED CORP. STRATEGY
Who controls strategy & plans?	SBU	mainly SBU with some MO influence	control shared: SBU & MO; MO ultimately controls resources & organization
Who owns profits/sur-pluses & determines re-investments	SBU	MO Corporate	MO Corporate
What is the nature of MO strategy/plans?	sum of SBU strategy/plans	more than sum SBU strategy/plans	much more than sum of SBU strategies & plans
What is the focus of MO strategy?	acquisitions/divest-ments to improve portfolio mix	resource allocation SBU management acquisitions divestitures	resource allocation, SBU management, inter-SBU synergy, acquisitions, divestitures image
What is the nature/size of MO staff?	minimal	moderate: a few enabling functions	strong: full range of enabling functions (i.e. HR, Finance, R&D, Info Services, Planning)
What is typical managing style of MO executives?	laissez-faire except when SBU performs poorly	controlling by the numbers	strong leadership but also with high degree of participation & collaboration: MO with SBUs
What is the need for conflict resolution & conflict management?	little	moderate	high
What is the importance of SONG?	important for SBUs but only moderately useful for MO as a whole	important for both SBUs & MO primary focus on the numbers	critically important for MO & SBUs; core process for managing the entire organization; both qualitative & quantitative

any profits/surplus and determines resource allocation and organization. Corporate, Group and SBU managers rely heavily on SONG both to run each SBU and to formulate and execute *corporate* strategy. Corporate is concerned not only with financial performance, but also with strategic positioning. An impor-tant aim is ensuring that the entire organization adds up to much more than simply the sum of its (SBU) parts. Examples of large MOs whose posture is at this end of the spectrum are General Electric and Motorola.

Somewhere between the holding company and integrated corporate strategy models on the MO posture spectrum is the *portfolio management model.* Here, Corporate leadership's relationship with its SBUs is somewhat more arm's length than in the integrated corporate strategy model, but is more involved than in the holding company model. Any SBU profits/surplus are "owned" and reallocated by Corporate. Its concerns are primarily with financial performance and with achieving an optimally structured portfolio. SBUs have a high degree of autonomy. Efforts to achieve cross-SBU synergies are modest. In my experience, the portfolio management model is the one most prevalent in MOs.

Factors Influencing Choice of MO Posture

Whatever model MO leaders choose as a posture, it is important to recognize that the performance of the organization as a whole depends first and foremost on how well its constituent SBUs perform. This performance is determined to a large extent by how effectively SBUs use SONG. Is this best left entirely to SBU management? To what extent can corporate executives help improve this practice? In Figure 8 is depicted the mix of Corporate/SBU influence on SBU strategy for the various models across the posture spectrum. As one moves to the right on this spectrum, the potential for conflict between SBUs and Corporate increases substantially. Figure 9 shows the potential area of conflict as corporate executives intervene in SBU strategy.

MO corporate leaders have a choice as to where on the posture spectrum they want to position their organization. Two considerations are paramount. One is the nature of the portfolio of SBUs … how many and how related are their businesses? When the number is relatively small and the businesses are related, there are often considerable opportunities for synergy and leveraging of capabilities across SBUs. With the integrated strategy model, the whole could be made much more than simply the sum of its (SBU) parts. This is far more difficult to achieve when the portfolio is comprised of many unrelated businesses. In this case, the portfolio management or holding company models are probably more feasible.

The other consideration is management's appetite for and competence in managing conflict. Conflict is inherent as SONG is used in MOs. There is conflict when SBUs compete for resources. There is potential conflict between SBU and Corporate executives in setting objectives, strategies and priorities. In the integrated corporate strategy model, because of the highly pro-active role taken by corporate executives in relation to SBUs, there is greater potential for conflict here than in the portfolio management and holding company models.

Figure 8
MIX OF MO/SBU INFLUENCE ON SBU STRATEGY

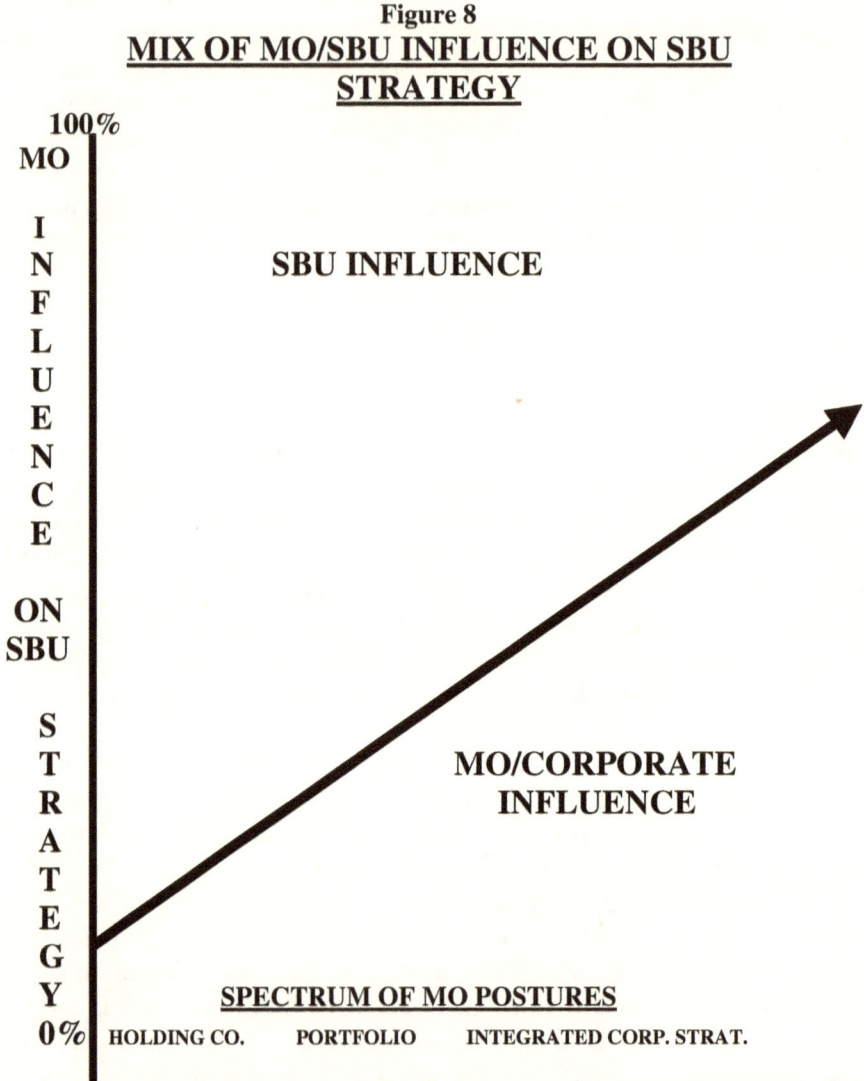

Figure 9
WHO CONTROLS SBU STRATEGY IN AN MO?

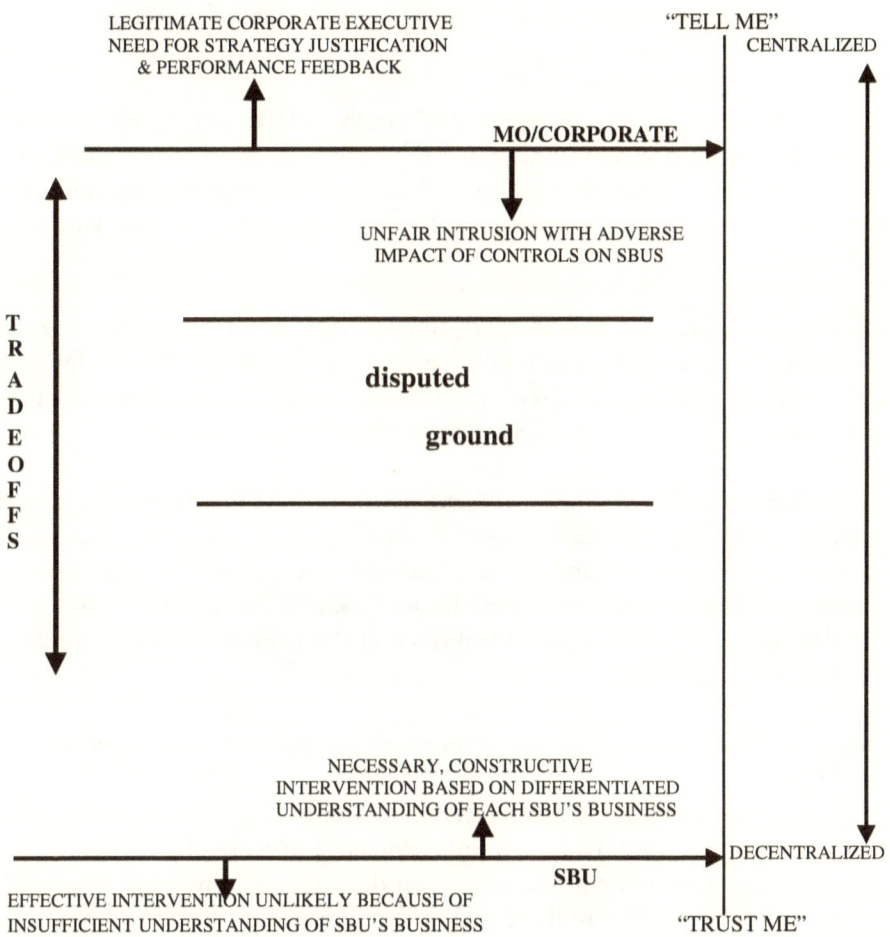

Corporate leaders must balance these two considerations in their choice of posture. Each model has its advantages and disadvantages. There is no 'best" or "right" answer. *What is crucial is that the choice be made consciously and deliberately, and that everyone concerned understand and buy-into the decision.* Furthermore, the implications of that decision must be articulated in the form of operating ground rules to be applied as SONG is used throughout the organization.

Principles of Effective Use of SONG in MOs

Whichever model corporate executives choose, effective use of SONG is based on the following nine fundamental principles:

1. The basic challenge is how to enable each SBU to engage its particular external environment effectively, and still achieve the kind of overall balance (e.g. growth vs. returns; resource utilization), synergy and optimization (investment vs. performance) required by corporate executives to execute their strategy.

2. The choice between centralization and decentralization is a red herring. It's better to determine which aspects of decision-making in an MO call for *integration* and which ones call for *differentiation*. Integration recognizes the interdependence among SBUs; differentiation respects their diversity.

3. Each SBU and its business needs are defined from an *outside perspective* of market-, customer- and competitor- centered analysis … not from the inside perspective of products and services, facilities, technology or organizational symmetry. The boundaries and definition of each SBU and its business should be determined by these external realities and the requirements and ramifications of the strategies it seeks to implement.

4. An MO's mission and strategy requires an *integrated overview* at the top, in order to:
> • maintain a risk/return equilibrium;
> • maintain a long-term regenerative or renewal process;
> • maintain a balance of asset deployment in terms of the overall portfolio profile of risk, industry maturity and competitive position; and
> • resolve tradeoff questions generated by the competing aspirations of SBUs, before MO resources can be properly allocated to their strategies.

5. SBU strategies must be *differentiated within general guidelines* (expected roles, contributions, constraints) reflecting the corporate executives' overview and strategy. This need arises from differences in:
> • the competitive dynamics in which the various SBUs are engaged;

- the capital intensity and maturity of the industries in which they participate;
- their market position and product/service quality; and
- the strategic roles they are performing for the MO (i.e. agents of growth and renewal, generators of cash, major sources of MO profits/surplus).

6. To support differentiated SBU strategies, it is necessary to permit *variations in the organizational and management framework* within which they operate, including appropriate variations in management style, and systems of control, compensation and information. Forced homogenization combined with undifferentiated bottom-line performance demands, can cripple many strategies from the start, or even preclude their getting started at all.

7. Any debate about whether planning should be top/down or bottom/up poses the wrong choice. Strategic and operational planning are better seen as both ... an iterative, cycling process where initial preliminary high-level concepts are tested and refined (or revised) by more concrete, detailed lower-level inputs.

8. Effective application of SONG requires an integration and close alignment among the eleven elements discussed in Chapters 6 and 7, and seven additional elements required for MOs (discussed in Chapter 9).

9. The best way to reconcile the strategies proposed by SBUs into a coherent MO strategy is not through a sequence of one-on-one presentations and reviews conducted in a propose/dispose mode. Instead, reconciliation should be achieved through a carefully structured process that brings the corporate executive team and all SBU and functional chiefs together at one time and place to achieve corporate integration and balance through constructive tension and conflict resolution. A vigorous and open, but structured, tradeoff debate conducted in a common language (I call this a Scrum) accomplishes the necessary reconciliation and integration while building understanding, commitment and motivation among all the key players at both Corporate and SBU levels (this process is discussed further in Chapter 9) ..

Two Fundamental Dilemmas

As SONG is applied in an MO, management must recognize and address two fundamental dilemmas. One stems from the reality that only SBUs generate revenues and profits/surpluses. Hence, only an SBU can be accountable for formulating and executing its business strategy. Yet, corporate executives are the ones who typically decide how much actually to provide of the resources needed to fund each SBU's intended strategy.

When the model for an MO's posture is integrated corporate strategy or portfolio management, only corporate executives determine how MO resources are to be allocated among several SBUs. This decision is especially critical when SBUs' aggregate requests for resources exceed what is available. Whatever their posture, only corporate executives ultimately determine which businesses the MO will be conducting, and how each is defined and organized … the actual makeup of the portfolio. How then can an SBU's management be truly accountable for delivering revenues and profits to the MO when it does not have full control over how its business is defined, how its SBU is structured and how MO resources are allocated?

The other dilemma has to do with MO/Corporate strategy. An MO's strategy is not simply an aggregation of the strategies of its constituent SBUs. Rather, MO strategy is concerned with such meta-strategic issues as what kinds of businesses it wants to conduct, the extent and rate of MO growth, the extent and nature of diversification, how much globalization, and (for organizations in the for-profit sector) growth of shareholder value. MO strategies required to address such issues transcend strategies executed by individual SBUs .SBU strategies must serve the interests of these MO strategies.

Thus, in order for SONG to work effectively in an MO, the interests, concerns, and objectives of corporate executives must mesh and be reconciled with the interests, concerns and objectives of the managements of each SBU. Any unresolved conflict can become a major obstacle to successful strategy implementation. SBU managers become demotivated and the entire planning and implementation process loses credibility.

MO strategy cannot be formulated until corporate executives know what possibilities and promises are embedded collectively in all of the SBUs' strategic plans. But if these strategic plans are to be soundly based and realistic, they must be formulated with a prior understanding of what levels of performance corporate executives want and are expecting from each SBU. SBU managers also need to know what resources they can reasonably expect to be allocated by the MO. This is the classic chicken-and-egg conundrum.

In Conclusion

The issues raised here are knotty and not readily resolved. Yet in order for an MO's management to realize the full potential power of SONG, it must make the effort to wrestle with these questions and pin down some answers. Most importantly, it must translate its answers explicitly into a set of ground rules for using SONG. In particular, these ground rules should clarify how the SBUs, Corporate Enabling or Support Functions, Operating Units, and Corporate executives should inter-relate and interact with one another in the setting of objectives, formulation and execution of strategy, setting of priorities, allocation of resources, tracking and monitoring implementation and the like.

How management chooses to answer these questions at the outset, need not be regarded as an irrevocable decision. As management gains experience in its use of SONG within a framework of explicit ground rules, it should remain flexible to modify or revise its posture and answers later on.

CHAPTER 9

HOW SONG WORKS IN MUTI-BUSINESS ORGANIZATIONS

In a single-business organization, management uses SONG to guide and control the setting and attainment of strategic objectives for the SBU. Typically this is the entire organization. Included are the operating system(s) that support the business strategy. Here, SONG operates at only one level ... that of the SBU.

In multi-business organizations (MOs), SONG operates at two and sometimes three levels. These are SBUs, MO/Corporate, and sometimes (in very large organizations with many SBUs) an intermediate Group level. An MO's SONG must simultaneously meet SBU and MO/Corporate needs which coincide in some respects and differ in others (see Chapter 8). In addition, an MO's SONG must help corporate executives and SBU managers reconcile any conflicts in objectives, priorities and agendas. In this chapter, I discuss the special characteristics of SONGs in MOs. Most of this discussion is concerned with two-level SONGs. At the end of the chapter, I address the special case of a three-level SONG.

Differences in the Eleven Basic SONG Elements

The eleven SONG elements discussed in Chapters 6 and 7 are part of, and work in an MO's SONG in very much the same way as they do in a single-business organization. There are, however, a few important differences described below.

1. Business Definition: no difference.

2. Definition of SBUs and OUs: no difference. In MOs, this element is especially important because it determines the number of SBUs and thus the complexity of SONG.

3. CEO's Provisional Strategic Guidelines: all the points discussed in Chapters 6 and 7 apply to MOs. However, everything contained in the document refers to the MO as a whole, not to any particular SBU (although the CEO might note certain issues and constraints relevant to particular SBUs). Thus, the CEO discusses objectives, constraints, values, performance, etc. for the entire organization.

An especially important discussion is about any resource constraints. The SBUs need to know before they begin formulating their Strategic Business Plans how difficult (or easy) it will be to get whatever resources they will need to execute their plans. With this knowledge, an SBU's Planning Group (PG) ensures clear, sound rationales for its Strategy Proposals (see next section) and sufficient justification for any requests for resources.

Another important section is the one dealing with key assumptions and compelling facts about the external environment. By providing these in the Guidelines, all the MO's SBUs use a common framework of shared assumptions and facts as they develop their plans .

The CEO's Provisional Guidelines Statement also contains important additional material dealing with MO/Corporate strategy as distinct from SBU strategies. This is in fact, an additional element peculiar to MOs' SONGs. The work to develop this element's content is distinct. The output from this work is integrated initially into the Provisional Guideline Statement. Later, it is distributed in the *CEO's Definitive Strategic Guidelines* (see element 12 in the following section).

In the Provisional Guideline Statement, the CEO outlines the MO's strategic objectives and strategies. Also, the *roles and contributions expected* of each SBU are made explicit. For example, SBUs 1 and 4 are expected to be the primary generators of profits or surplus, SBUs 2 and 3 are expected to be the major sources of revenue growth, SBU 5 is looked to as a prime source of innovation, SBUs 6 and 8 are expected to contribute the most to cash flow, SBU 7 is expected to be the node for diversification into new businesses, and so on. By signaling each SBU what role it is expected to play in the total MO portfolio, and the contribution it is expected to make to MO/Corporate performance, the SBU's PG can begin its work of formulating its Strategic Business Plan with a clear understanding of what it must deliver. It knows from the outset how ambitious should be its objectives, how much risk will be accepted and how demanding it could be regarding resources.

4. Base Future Scenario: no difference. As the management team performing this task draws members from several SBUs and Corporate Enabling Functions, its perspective is likely to be broader than that of a group drawn from a single SBU.

5. SBU's Strategic Business Plan: A key difference from the element described in Chapters 6 and 7 is that in MOs, the initial output of the strategic planning process is an *SBU Strategy Proposal*, not a validated plan (this comes later after the Scrum described in the following section). The process for developing the Strategy Proposal is essentially the same as that described in Chapter 6. The SBU Strategy Proposal is element 13, one of seven additional MO SONG elements discussed in the following section.

6. Operating Plan(s): no difference in Operating Plans that directly support each SBU's Strategic Business Plan. There is a key difference for MOs' major Corporate Enabling/Support Functions (e.g. Human Resources, Information Services, Finance, etc.). When such corporate functions are large, they formulate their own Operating Plans distinct from those addressing SBUs' operating systems. Prior to this, however, they also formulate a Corporate Function Operating Plan Proposal as an input to the Corporate Scrum. This is element 14, one the seven additional MO SONG elements discussed below.

7. Process for Performance Measurement, Monitoring Implementation Progress and Updating Strategic and Operating Plans: no difference.

8. Strategically-Driven Financial Plan and Budget: no difference.

9. Strategically-Driven Compensation and Rewards: no difference, except that in very large MOs with large SBUs, there may be some variation in the particulars of compensation from one SBU to another, to enable tailoring of the reward system to each specific SBU's situation and strategy.

10. Strategically-Driven MIS: no difference, except that the system must accommodate differentiated information requirements from one SBU to another.

11. Strategically-Driven Communications: no difference.

Additional SONG Elements for MOs

For SONG to be useful in an MO, it must have seven additional elements to the eleven already discussed.

12. Corporate Objectives, Expectations and Strategies

Over and beyond the strategic objectives and plans of its constituent SBUs, an MO has its own set of *corporate* objectives, strategies and expectations of its SBUs. These are distinct and different from those of any single SBU.

> For example, a large social agency, Morgan Memorial Goodwill Industries (MMGI) conducts several different "businesses". One collects donated clothing and household goods and sells them at nominal prices through a chain of its own retail outlets. Another "business" operates camps for adults and children primarily from inner city areas. Yet another "business" provides vocational counseling and training aimed at helping clients find employment. MMGI is an MO. Each of its businesses/SBUs has its own strategic plan. But MMGI has separate corporate strategic objectives and strategies. One is aimed at enhancing Goodwill's image and recognition in the community ... an important prerequisite to successful fund raising. Another is aimed at seeking other social agencies as candidates either for strategic alliances or merger partners ... a means of strengthening existing programs and diversifying into new ones.

Corporate objectives and strategies generally fall into four broad categories. One has to do with changing the nature of the portfolio of businesses. Another has to do with improving the MO's corporate performance with the existing portfolio. A third category has to do with changing the geographic scope of the MO's businesses and operations. The fourth aims at ensuring the long-term viability and vitality of the MO as an entity.

Here are some examples of corporate strategies.

-   Changing the portfolio of businesses

- Acquisitions and/or divestitures to diversify into new industries, or to exit some industries … to change the mix of businesses in the portfolio … to shift the balance towards more revenue growth, towards more cash generation or profit, towards more or less diversity, etc.
- Improving corporate performance
- Reallocating resources among existing SBUs to accelerate the execution of those SBU strategies that directly impact shareholder value (for MOs in the profit sector), or that have the biggest impact on the achievement of other corporate objectives (e.g. enhancing the MO's visibility and image, attracting new funders, avoidance of takeovers, etc.).
- Changing geographic scope
- Expanding existing businesses and operations from local to regional, from regional to national, from national to international, from international to global (or narrowing scope in the reverse direction) by joint ventures, strategic alliances, acquisitions and divestitures and by entering new businesses in other localities, either by direct investment, or by joint ventures, alliances, etc.
- Ensuring long-term viability and vitality
- Investing within the MO in research and development, management and employee training and development, productivity improvement and organizational effectiveness, process innovation, information technology, upgrading facilities and equipment, etc.… to sustain a process of organizational renewal in an ever-changing external environment.

Setting strategic objectives for an MO and choosing strategies to achieve them is work for corporate executives, with the CEO playing the lead role. These objectives reflect the vision of the MO's leadership, and should also be sensitive to the needs and interests of the MO's other stakeholders (see Chapter 4).

Initially, an MO's leaders cannot know whether or not the strategic objectives and strategies they select are realistically achievable. The answer to this question becomes apparent only after the SBUs complete their strategy proposals and the outcomes promised are aggregated and reviewed, along with the resources requested to support strategy execution. If the collective results promised fall short of the intended corporate objectives, or if the aggregate resources required are beyond the MO's capabilities to provide them, MO executives have but two alternatives. They can ask SBUs to "go back to the drawing board" and try again to formulate more powerful SBU strategies. Or they can set less ambitious objectives for the MO.

Only after at least one iteration of this process can definitive MO corporate objectives and strategies be set. This is why initial corporate objectives and strategies are incorporated into the CEO's Provisional Strategic Guidelines. Later, after the Corporate Scrum (see element 17 below) the CEO makes any needed modifications to the corporate objectives and strategies and distributes a *Definitive Strategic Guideline Statement.*.

13. SBU Strategy Proposals

With the CEO's Provisional Strategic Guidelines as a starting point, each of the MO's SBUs forms a Planning Group (PG) to formulate a *proposed* SBU Strategic Business Plan as described in Chapter 6, Section 5. The process for Phase 1, selecting the foundation strategies, is identical. The major work in Phase 2, developing an action program and an accompanying measurement and monitoring plan may be somewhat less intensive and complete than what was described in Chapter 6. The PG does sufficient action planning to validate its choices of strategy, to lend credibility to these choices and to identify the resources required to execute its proposed plan.

The final product of the PG's work is a SBU Strategy Proposal. This is a principal input for the Corporate Interrogation (see 15 below) and the Corporate Scrum (see 17 below).

Here is a typical format for an SBU Strategy Proposal. It is important that every SBU in an MO use the same format, because this eases the work done in the Corporate Interrogation, the Portfolio Analysis and in the Corporate Scrum (elements 15. 16 and 17 below).

1. SBU Profile

- Current scope of the business depicted in one or more matrices showing revenues by market offering by distribution channel, number of customers by geographic area accounting for 80% of revenues, etc.

- SBU's contribution to the MO … by revenues, profits/surplus, assets and employees

- SBU's capacity utilization … average annual number over past several years

2. Business Definition

3. Industry Characterization: principal segments, size and expected growth, nature and drivers of customer expenditures, key trends (by geography) that impact business, any seasonality or cyclicality

4. Market Characterization: customer classes and needs by geography, market size and projected growth, market shares, distribution channels and needs, relative stability of markets served

5. Competitive Analysis

- Existing and potential customers' future needs vs. SBU's current market offerings
- Principal competitors, market shares and bases of competition (by geography)
- SBU's competitive strengths and weaknesses
- Key success factors

6. Key Proposed Objectives, Strategies and Programs

- Key strategic issues
- Strategic objectives
- Principal strategies and focus ... summary of major programs for each strategy.
- Key business processes

7. Bases for Successful Strategy Execution

- Key dependencies
- Use of resources
- Key disinvestments

8. Financial Summary

- Promised performance
- Required resources

9. Key Assumptions and Risk Analysis

An SBU's Strategy Proposal differs from a Strategic Business Plan in the level of detail included. This is because the purposes of these two documents are different. An SBU's Strategy Proposal should contain sufficient information to enable corporate executives and other SBU heads to understand the intended strategy and the *gross* projected outcomes and resource requirements. The Proposal should contain sufficient information not only to ensure this understanding but also to enable executives outside the SBU to assess the credibility of the intended strategy and its promised results. By contrast, a Strategic Business Plan enables everyone accountable, involved and impacted by the plan to understand not only what the SBU is intending to achieve, how and why, but also what *they* are required to do differently to assure successful plan execution. Because of these differences in purpose, a Strategy Proposal is more "broad brush" and contains less detail than a Strategic Business Plan. This applies both to qualitative characterizations and explanations, and to quantitative projections of performance and resource requirements.

14. Corporate Function Operating Plan Proposals

Like SBUs, major Corporate Enabling/Supporting Functions are substantial consumers of an MO's resources. In very large MOs, these functions are most typically Finance, Information Services/Technology, Human Resources, Research and Development and possibly Corporate Planning/Development and Legal.

These functions not only support each SBU's strategy, but also they often plan and implement *corporate* programs that apply to all SBUs. For example, Information Services/Technology may lead a corporate effort to upgrade information technology throughout the MO, introducing new systems to support integrated cross-functional business processes such as new product development and order-to-delivery. Human Resources may lead a corporate effort to institute a more systematic approach to management succession and development or to develop a comprehensive employee database. Finance may lead a corporate effort to introduce strategy-driven budgeting.

Thus, each major Corporate Function formulates and implements its own Proposed Operating Plan. But this plan cannot be definite until corporate executives approve it and allocate the required resources. Before they can do this, they must consider Corporate Functions together with their SBUs as they make resource allocation decisions. Such consideration occurs during and immediately after the Corporate Scrum (element 17 below), and requires the submission beforehand of a Corporate Function Operating Plan Proposal (CFOPP).

Like SBU Strategy Proposals, CFOPPs are meant to inform corporate executives and SBU leadership of each Corporate Function's intended objectives, plans, resource requirements and promised outcomes, along with a supporting rationale. The process for formulating a CFOPP is similar to that described for Operating Plans in Chapter 6. Each Corporate Function forms an Operating Planning Group (OPG). Its work in Phase 1 to select the plan's foundation strategies is essentially the same as that described in Chapter 6. Its work in Phase 2 to formulate detailed action plans and measures is less intensive and detailed, as is the case for SBU Strategy Proposals.

Here is a typical format for a CFOPP. As in the case for SBU Strategy Proposals. it is important to use a uniform format for the same reasons described in the preceding section.

1. Profile of the Corporate Function

- summary/overview of current "business" showing the % resources allocated to providing categories of services to SBUs and to MO Corporate
- function's mission and role regarding customers, services and focus

2. Professional Developments Impacting the Function: developments and trends (e.g. technology, new concepts, methods and practices, etc.) that may impact future expenditures

3. Customer Characterization: current and unmet needs

4. Priorities: relative to SBU and MO plans

5. Key Proposed Functional Objectives, Strategies and Programs

- key operational issues
- functional objectives (operational, services provided, financial)
- strategies and focus (see Appendix C) plus major supporting pro-grams
- key business processes that create value for customers; level of com-petence; contribution to plan's success

6. Bases for Successful Plan Execution

- key dependencies for plan's success
- resource utilization, including any critical investment dependencies
- disinvestments

7. Financial Summary: projected financial outcomes and resource requirements

8. Key Assumptions and Risk Analysis

A CFOPP differs from an Operating Plan in the level of detail provided. As with SBU Strategy Proposals, a CFOPP's purpose differs from that of Operating Plans. These inform everyone involved with implementation what they must do, how, when, why, and who is accountable. A CFOPP informs MO executives and SBU heads of the function's intended objectives and plans and what resources it needs and why. Just enough information should be included to make the case.

15. Corporate Interrogation of SBU Strategy Proposals

This and the next two additional SONG elements help corporate executives and SBU management reconcile and align MO/Corporate and each SBU's interests with regard to objectives, strategies, priorities and resources. The first of these is a formal interaction between corporate executives and senior managers from each SBU *separately*. Requiring typically a half-day with each SBU, this element is a Corporate Interrogation of each SBU's Strategy Proposal.

Corporate Interrogation has three purposes. One is to ensure that corporate executives understand each SBU's proposed strategy along with its underlying rationale. Interrogation provides corporate executives an opportunity to ask questions about every aspect of each proposal to elicit more information. Another aim is to enable corporate executives to test each proposal's credibility by probing with further questioning, and assessing its strengths and weaknesses. A third aim is to clarify and strengthen each SBU's Strategy Proposal in anticipation of the Corporate Scrum (Section 16 below).

During Interrogation, corporate executives may test ideas for possible improvements to strengthen a strategy proposal. Often these suggested modifications are aimed at clarifying language that may be ambiguous or confusing, and providing additional information to fill in gaps. Sometimes, suggestions are aimed at strengthening the rationale for the proposed strategy. Seldom are suggestions offered to change the proposed strategy.

Here is how Corporate Interrogation works. Corporate executives receive an SBU's Strategy Proposal at least two weeks in advance of the scheduled Interrogation. This enables them to study the proposal and formulate questions in advance of the meeting. Typically, Interrogation begins with a formal presentation by the SBU's senior management team of their proposed strategy's highlights including the supporting rationale. This presentation is limited to 20 minutes. In the remaining 2.5–3.0 hours, Corporate executives ask questions and listen to SBU managers' responses until they are satisfied that all their questions and concerns have received responses. Then they ask SBU managers to leave the meeting. Corporate executives continue to discuss and agree on any suggested modifications to the Strategy Proposal. Typically these are offered within a week of Interrogation.

Questions asked by corporate executives tend to address several different concerns. One is the relationship between specific aspects of the SBU's Strategy Proposal and how the SBU intends to apply resources. Corporate executives need to understand the impact of any changes they might make later on in resource allocation. Another concern is the credibility of any promises for future improvement in SBU performance. This is addressed by questions probing the reasons for any past variances in the SBU's past promises versus actual performance.

Corporate executives need to probe the SBU team to ensure understanding of what distinguishes that SBU's business and business environment from those of other SBUs. Are there any unique characteristics that require Corporate to tailor its expectations of performance and its allocation of resources? Corporate executives need to know what information is critical. They need to feel comfortable with how the SBU is defining its business.

There are questions about what is critical to successful strategy execution. Are there any corporate policies and procedures that might be obstacles and need modification? What special help is needed from Corporate Enabling/Support Functions? Are executive and managerial incentives sufficient and appropriate?

Corporate executives need to feel comfortable that corporate objectives, priorities and resources are truly reflected in the SBU's Strategy Proposal. They also need to be satisfied that the SBU's key strategic issues are suitably addressed by the proposed strategies, that the proposed action program is sufficient and credible, and that the key assumptions and risk analysis are realistic.

Interrogation helps corporate executives better understand and become more sensitive to and comfortable with each SBU's situation, business, intentions, promises and needs. This process also stimulates improvement both of SBU Strategy Proposals and of corporate policies, procedures and support. It is an important means for moving toward closer alignment between Corporate and SBU interests and concerns.

16. Portfolio Analysis

This additional element of an MO's SONG is an important input for the Corporate Scrum, typically prepared by Corporate Finance working with Corporate Planning. It consists of various cross-sectional analyses of the corporation's portfolio of SBUs, prepared prior to the Scrum. These analyses show on a series of trend charts, performance data in various dimensions, for the MO in its entirety and by SBU, both retrospectively and prospectively. Past performance is actual. Projected performance is derived from SBUs' promises and resource demands as documented in SBU Strategy Proposals and CFOPPs.

The intent is to illuminate the aggregate impact of SBUs' proposed strategies on the MO, so that both their adequacy in meeting corporate objectives and Corporate's ability to provide needed resources can be assessed. The portfolio analysis also enables scrum participants to take a corporate perspective and understand their relationship and contribution to the MO as a whole.

A portfolio analysis also enables the identification of any issues important to the organization as a whole. For example, how much of a gap is there between the aggregate promises of improved SBUs' performance and the MO's strategic objectives? How much of a gap is there between SBUs' and Corporate Functions' aggregate resource demands and resources available? To what extent do SBUs' proposed strategies improve the MO's competitive strength and how? To what extent do SBUs' proposed strategies increase risk for the MO, and in what way?

Here are examples of the kinds of exhibits included in a portfolio analysis.

Financial Performance

- revenues: total MO, and by SBU
- assets: total MO, and by SBU
- rate of MO revenue and asset growth
- rate of revenue and asset growth by SBU
- % revenues and assets by SBU

Value Creation

- after tax profits/surplus: total MO, and by SBU
- earnings per share
- after tax profit/surplus growth rate: total MO, and by SBU
- % after tax profits/surplus by SBU
- book value: corporation, and by SBU: actual and % of MO
- return on equity: MO, and by SBU
- profitability matrix: earnings growth vs. average % return on equity
- cash flow and total investment
- portfolio value growth rate
- value creation by SBU
- rate of value creation by SBU
- growth per unit of currency of value as of selected date
- rate of after tax earning growth by SBU
- average return on equity by SBU
- rate of operating cash flow growth by SBU
- value contribution by SBU

Qualitative improvements in strategic position by SBU (future only)

- earnings stability (risk)
- health and safety risk

- environmental risk
- relative share of market (vs. competitors)
- relative costs (vs. competitors)
- relative quality (vs. competitors)
- relative competitive strength

A portfolio analysis is not distributed in advance. Rather it is presented at the Scrum. This is because some of the charts presented require explanation and elaboration. The overall impact is powerful. Many questions are generated. An MO-wide view is stimulated. Perceptions of SBUs' roles in and contributions to the MO frequently change. Strategic issues for the MO snap into focus.

17. Corporate Scrum

MOs' Have the Gordian Knot Problem

In MOs, there is a unique issue of exceptional importance. How it is resolved determines whether SONG delivers its full potential. This issue is as challenging as the fabled Gordian Knot: how can management reconcile and align inescapable differences between Corporate and SBUs with regard to objectives, strategies, priorities and resources?

These differences arise because Corporate's and SBUs' functions and agendas are profoundly different. On the one hand, only SBUs generate revenues and profits, based on how they utilize assets and resources. Each SBU determines how to optimize performance both near- and long-term. On the other hand, Corporate determine which businesses it wants to be in, and how to make its portfolio add up to more than simply the sum of its SBU parts. Corporate decides how resources are to be allocated among SBUs and for acquisitions, and how to promote and capitalize on opportunities for leverage and synergy. Despite these differences, it is the interdependency of Corporate and SBUs that drives achievement of both Corporate and SBU strategic objectives.

Typically, this combination of interdependency and differences in function and agendas can give rise to a number of *corporate* complaints and concerns that adversely affect the relationship between Corporate and SBUs. These complaints and concerns tend to show up in five areas: (1) problems with numbers; (2) problems with information; (3) problems with motivation; (4) distortions; and (5) chronic disappointments.

In the area of numbers, Corporate often feels frustrated. When reviewing aggregated numbers accompanying an SBU's Strategy Proposal, Corporate often has difficulty assessing the impact of events and of changed assumptions. When reviewing aggregated numbers in reports of SBU performance, Corporate typically has trouble understanding the causes of variances. Also, numbers accompanying an SBU's Strategy Proposal often are puffed up in anticipation of Corporate discounts or mandated cuts, and may be hiding subjective estimates of risk and uncertainty.

In the area of information, Corporate often feels inundated in a sea of data, wondering what's *really* important. Also, Corporate often feels uneasy that it is not getting the really critical information for the particular business under review.

In the area of motivation, Corporate typically agonizes over how to answer three key questions about its relationship with SBUs. How far should we encourage internal competition for resources to sharpen and motivate managers ... without undermining cooperation and coordination? How credible is the "entrepreneurship" we're trying to cultivate in SBUs, when their plans are usually revised after our reviews? Should we risk killing motivation in the SBUs with centralized constraints and controls, or allow parochial interests to predominate under a more decentralized approach?

Corporate also wrestles with the problem of how to minimize distortions characteristic in MOs. For example, each SBU has a stake in emphasizing its unique situation and "selling"its plan separately to compete for corporate resources. By contrast, Corporate often has uniform expectations of dissimilar SBUs. Corporate functions often "goldplate" their services and organizations, a tendency supported by mutual deference among "experts". SBUs' plans, priorities and resource requirements are often misaligned with corporate objectives, priorities and resources.

Then there are chronic disappointments that affect both Corporate and SBUs. All too often, unexpected external events overtake even well formulated plans. SBUs' plans often project J-curves that depend more on loyalty, hard work, technical know-how and power than on sound strategy. And SBUs' implementation of strategies often fall apart because action plans are inadequately detailed and explicit, and supervisors and lower level managers lack understanding and commitment, or because management's attention and focus is diverted or diluted.

Typical Approaches to Dealing with the Gordian Knot

Historically, MOs have taken three approaches to deal with the Gordian Knot issue. One is a sequence of SBU presentations to Corporate followed by interrogation. Resource allocation decisions are then made individually for each SBU in a propose/dispose mode. Another less formal approach is interactions, negotiations and deals done one-at-a-time and separately, between an SBU head and one or more Corporate chiefs. A third approach has been uniform, often arbitrary, across-the-board cuts in allocated resources to all SBUs mandated by Corporate.

All three approaches are seriously flawed, often undermining the effectiveness of strategic planning and implementation. An SBU head may get Corporate to provide desired resources by effective selling or successful lobbying, whether in a formal presentation or in a one-on-one deal. When this happens, other SBUs with possibly better prospects but less adept in persuasion, may get short-changed to the detriment of the MO as a whole. When aggregate SBUs' demand for resources exceeds what is available, Corporate may "solve" the problem by mandating uniform across-the-board cuts for all SBUs. This ignores valid differentiated SBU needs based on differences in circumstances, strategies and underlying rationales.

All three approaches result in misallocated resources. This seriously damages SBUs' ability to execute their strategies. Equally devastating, credibility of the entire strategic planning and implementation process is undermined, demotivating key SBU managers in their plan execution. These deficiencies in MO managements' efforts to resolve the crucial issue of reconciliation and alignment may help explain why so many MOs' performance is disappointing.

Cutting the Gordian Knot

For any approach to reconciliation and alignment to be free of these deficiencies, three criteria must be met. All SBUs' Strategy Proposals must be dealt with not sequentially but together at once. The differentiated circumstances, prospects and needs of each SBU must be taken into account and addressed. And the process must be credible and not demotivate the very SBU managers on whom corporate executives depend to deliver desired performance.

The Corporate Scrum (1) is a carefully structured process that brings corporate executives and all SBU and functional chiefs together at one time and place to achieve corporate integration and balance through constructive tension and conflict resolution. Vigorous, open but structured tradeoff debate is conducted in a common language. This has proven highly successful with several MOs in accomplishing required reconciliation, integration and alignment, while simultaneously building understanding, commitment and motivation among SBU managers.

Typically, a Corporate Scrum is an intensive working session lasting three full days in a comfortable off-site venue with 30–48 participants. It is not a decision-making event. Corporate executives make actual decisions about resource allocation and other corporate matters typically within 2–3 weeks *after* the Scrum. The Scrum provides an opportunity and forum for raising and discussing issues arising from close and comprehensive examination of SBUs' Strategy Proposals and CFOPPs in the context of corporate objectives and strategy. This discussion enables corporate executives subsequently to make better decisions. All Scrum participants also better understand the rationale underlying resource allocation decisions, minimizing any potential demotivation.

There are five objectives for a Corporate Scrum:

1. to improve subsequent resource allocation decisions so that these support those SBUs with the best prospects for performance and alignment with corporate goals, not those with the most attractive sales pitches;

2. to strengthen the case for either maintaining or changing the makeup of the MO's portfolio of SBUs;

3. to build understanding, consensus and support (especially among SBU heads) for subsequent resource allocation and other corporate executive decisions;

4. to identify and address any critical MO issues; and

5. to identify and address any cross-SBU opportunities both for leveraging particular technical or organizational capabilities and for potential synergies.

In my experience designing and conducting scrums, not only have all five of these objectives invariably been achieved, but also participants gained an additional major benefit. They learned a great deal about what the other SBUs were doing and were intending to do in the future. Also, they acquired a much better understanding of corporate objectives, strategy and underlying rationales.

A Corporate Scrum's effectiveness in achieving these five objectives depends on how well management deals with four issues. Are the "right" participants involved? Are the inputs prepared in advance for the scrum complete, soundly conceived and well presented? Are the facilities, logistics and process designed to support fruitful discussion and desired outcomes? Does corporate executive behavior encourage honesty, openness and personal risk-taking? How each of these issues can best be addressed is discussed in turn below.

The "Right" Participants

In every Scrum, three constituencies are represented … Corporate, SBUs and Corporate Enabling/support Functions. Typically, Corporate is represented by the CEO and his/her direct reports. Each SBU is represented by at least the SBU head, and if numbers permit (see following discussion), 1–3 of his/her key reports. Each Corporate Enabling Function is represented by at least its head, and if numbers permit, 1–2 key reports.

In any Scrum, there is a trade-off between sufficient representation of each of these three constituencies, and a limit on the total number of participants in the interests of an environment conducive to productive discussion. In my experience the ideal total is between 30 and 36. I have, however, conducted highly successful scrums with as many as 48 participants.

When choices must be made to limit the total number, two criteria can be applied: importance to the MO, and personal ability to make useful contributions to Scrum discussions. How important to the MO's portfolio, now and later on, is the particular SBU? How critical to the MO's future success is a particular function? To what extent is the prospective participant likely to be open, forthcoming, forthright and likely to make constructive and creative contributions?

When the number of SBUs in an MO's portfolio is large (more than 8), it may be impossible in a single Scrum to address each SBU separately. In such instances, the portfolio is typically organized into groups of related SBUs, each reporting to a Group Executive. Each group conducts a Group Scrum prior to the Corporate Scrum to prepare a Group Strategy Proposal. At the Corporate Scrum, every Group is represented, but not necessarily every SBU; analysis, consideration and discussion is at Group rather than SBU level. Subsequent MO resource allocation is to Groups.

Inputs to the Scrum

Thorough preparation for the Scrum is vital. The quality of inputs prepared beforehand determines a Scrum's effectiveness. Quality means both the comprehensiveness and soundness of analysis and thought, and the way conclusions and supporting rationales are presented. These inputs are combined into a Scrum Workbook (typically 1.5–3 inches thick), sent to each participant at least ten days before the Scrum. Participants study this material prior to the Scrum and note questions and concerns. Formal presentations at the Scrum are minimized, allowing maximum time for discussion and interaction.

Each input should be self-explanatory, user-friendly and easily read. For SBU Strategy Proposals and CFOPPs, a uniform format is agreed in advance and followed. Explanatory templates are useful. The level of detail is that of a comprehensive executive summary. Succinctness and brevity is the rule. Just enough supporting data is included to lend credibility to analyses and conclusions. Inputs to a scrum include:

- CEO's Provisional Corporate Strategic Guidelines
- Alternative Base Future Scenarios
- SBU Strategy Proposals
- Enabling/support Functions' Proposed Operating Plans
- Portfolio Analysis
- Discussion Papers: Strategically important MO issues are discussed at a Scrum to promote broad understanding and encourage debate. For example, what problems do MO executives face in gaining access to capital markets? How is shareholder value defined, and what priority does this have in driving MO performance? What corporate capabilities are critical for future success, and what can be done to develop these? Are there weaknesses in the makeup of the portfolio, and what can be done to remedy these? For each such issue, a brief discussion paper is prepared in advance of the Scrum, posing the issue and its significance, and suggesting one or more possible approaches to its resolution, noting pros and cons for each one. No more than four discussion papers should be taken up in any single Scrum.

Facilities, Logistics and Process

Facilities, logistics and process for a Scrum are selected and designed to support and facilitate easy and open discussion among participants. The facility should be away from the corporate offices to minimize distractions and interruptions, and to enable an informal and relaxed setting and dress. A Scrum is best conducted in a large, airy meeting room with good sight lines and acoustics, that can accommodate up to 8 round tables each seating 6, a projector and screen, and 2–3 side tables for food and drink for continental breakfast and breaks, and for materials. Lunches and dinners are served in a separate room. If the facility is a resort hotel, additional time (beyond the 3 full days for the Scrum agenda) should be planned for recreation.

Participants are assigned comfortable chairs (padded with arms), 5–6 at a round table. Seating is configured to ensure that no one sits at the same table with his/her boss, and that representation is heterogeneous (multiple SBUs and Corporate Functions). The corporate executive team sits together at one table. The CEO is invited to roam and sit in wherever s/he likes. There is a flip chart, easel and thick felt-tipped marking pens at each table, and two such setups flanking the projector screen at the front of the room. Table seating configurations (other than the corporate executive team) can be changed each day to enable variety of inter-action.

Such a table arrangement has several advantages. It permits rapid and easy shifts from small- to full-group discussion modes. As each participant is part of a small group, s/he has much greater opportunity to participate than would be the case in a group of 36–48. Furthermore, by separating participants from their bosses, the environment is less threatening, more conducive to openness and forthright inputs. Also minimizing concerns about taking personal risks in speak-ing out, is the fact that inputs into the full group discussion are outputs of small *groups*. Thus, questions raised and concerns voiced are identified with a small group at a table, not an individual. This configuration enables widespread and fruitful participation, even when the full group size is large.

Another key to effective Scrums is a structured and disciplined process that maximizes discussion opportunities. This calls for a clear agenda, managed by a skilled facilitator whose sole objective is a fruitful discussion. A typical agenda has four segments.

First (1.5–2 hours), a framework or context is established for the Scrum. After brief introductory remarks from the CEO and facilitator to clarify objectives, expected outcomes and ground rules for participation, questions are encouraged about any aspect of the CEO's Provisional Corporate Strategic Guidelines. Next, there is a presentation of the Base Future Scenario(s) followed by a question period. If SBUs' aggregate demand for resources are likely to exceed what Corporate can provide, there may also be a presentation and discussion in the full group of criteria for assessing the relative attractiveness of SBU strategy proposals (Scrum participants are asked to assume the role of investment bankers who must decide on funding priorities when considering a group of SBU strategy proposals).

In the next agenda segment, which may extend into the afternoon of the sec-ond day, Scrum participants discuss in turn each SBU's (or Group's) Strategy Proposal. First there is a formal presentation (limited to 15 minutes) in which the salient elements of a proposed strategy are summarized. Next, each small group discusses and records on flip charts (for about 30 minutes) questions and con-cerns they may have about the proposed strategy, along with any issues for the MO. During this period, the facilitator develops a consolidated list of questions and concerns, and potential issues. This list serves as the agenda for a full group discussion that may take an additional 30–45 minutes. Potential MO issues agreed by the full group are recorded on another flip chart for consideration later on. For a single SBU or Group Strategy Proposal this process typically takes 1.7–2.0 hours.

After all strategy proposals have been thus taken up, the small groups and full group follow the same procedure for all CFOPPs considered together. This discussion may or may not be preceded by brief formal presentations, depending on time constraints.

The third agenda segment, which may extend into the morning of the third day, begins with presentation and discussion of the Portfolio Analysis. In this 1.5–2 hour module, the small group discussion process can be applied to raise questions and issues, followed by a full group discussion, recording any agreed issues. In the remainder of this segment, the discussion papers are taken up one by one with no presentations. Any issues for the MO agreed in the discussions are recorded.

The final agenda segment takes up most of the third day. It begins with small groups reviewing and prioritizing the list of potential MO issues, and the full group agreeing on a final prioritized list. Then there is a discussion of whether there should be any changes to the CEO's Provisional Corporate Guidelines in light of these issues and the preceding Scrum discussions. In the time remaining, each small group formulates proposed action plans for 1–2 assigned issues. Another task for this final segment might be the completion of a worksheet by each small group assessing relative attractiveness of SBU or Group Strategy Proposals applying the criteria agreed at the outset of the Scrum. At or immediately after the conclusion of the Scrum, the CEO assigns accountability for developing and executing action plans to resolve each issue.

Appropriate Corporate Executive Behavior

The fourth key success factor for an effective Scrum is appropriate behavior by the CEO and his/her reports. They must strike a delicate balance between listening and making forthright comments when appropriate. They should do everything possible to create an atmosphere that encourages and supports maximum open and honest participation by every Scrum participant.

After setting the stage, the CEO and his/her executive group should focus on listening. But when questions are raised calling for an answer or an expression of opinion from Corporate, the appropriate executive should respond in a way that does not shut down further discussion. If however, ideas arise that are clearly "out of bounds", the CEO should not shrink from reminding the group of any boundary conditions or constraints. To do otherwise would be dishonest, encouraging fruitless discussion.

Whenever several levels of management come together to debate the future of a business/organization, the quality of discussion is constrained by lower level managers not knowing where their bosses stand on certain matters. Often, much attention is paid to watching for signals from on high to divine which way the wind is blowing. When corporate executives provide answers, however unpopular, discussion is typically freed up rather than inhibited.

When corporate executives sit together at a single table during the Scrum, they can model behavior for everyone else. They can demonstrate openness, collaboration, creativity and unity of purpose. The CEO has a similar opportunity to demonstrate openness, listening, and forthrightness.

Outcomes From a Scrum

Typically a Scrum has six outcomes. Some strategies and plans proposed by SBUs and Corporate Functions are validated. Others are sent "back to the drawing board" for rework. Some proposed plans and programs are deferred or stopped. The makeup of the corporate portfolio is either validated or modified. A number of MO issues are identified and addressed: some are potential or actual problems; others are opportunities for improving corporate performance. Finally, everyone who participates learns a lot … about one another's businesses and plans, about the MO's prospects and strategy, and about how to improve SONG's effectiveness.

A Scrum is a process for ensuring alignment and balance between Corporate's and SBUs' interests in a way that ensures buy-in from the SBUs … the entities on which Corporate depends to achieve its strategic objectives. There are three reasons why a Scrum is far superior to alternative, more commonly used approaches to resource allocation in MOs. It minimizes any potentially demotivating impact on SBUs by Corporate's decisions. It ensures that "the right" issues get flushed out for Corporate's actions. And it ensures better resource allocation and thus the realization of the full potential power of SONG as a core process for running the enterprise.

18. Definitive Corporate Strategic Guidelines

The seventh additional MO SONG element is a Definitive Corporate Strategic Guideline Statement developed and distributed by the CEO within two to three weeks after the Corporate Scrum. This statement reflects discussions and any agreements reached at the Scrum. With the benefit of fresh insights and perspectives gained from the Scrum, the CEO and key corporate executives decide immediately afterwards, what changes to make in the CEO's Provisional Strategic Guidelines. They decide how to allocate Corporate's resources. They determine the changes required to SBU Strategy Proposals and CFOPPs to bring these into better alignment with Corporate's objectives and strategies. And they decide on which major MO issues agreed in the Scrum will be addressed, who will be accountable for resolving them, and when.

In the Definitive Corporate Strategic Guidelines, the CEO articulates MO objectives and strategies along with clear instructions to SBUs and Corporate Functions about required changes to their proposed strategies and plans. The Definitive Guidelines are explicit about how resources will be allocated ... which strategies and plans are approved, which must be abandoned, and which must be modified and how. Also included are any intended modifications to the MO's portfolio of SBUs, and a discussion of MO issues agreed at the Scrum and how these will be addressed.

How 18 Elements Work Together In An MO SONG In An Annual Cycle

Figure 10 shows how the eighteen SONG elements work together in an MO's planning cycle tuned to a calendar year. Elements are positioned as being the responsibility of Corporate, SBU, or a Corporate Function. When an element is shown under more than a single heading (e.g. Corporate Interrogation, Corporate Scrum, Implementation Measurement and Monitoring and Communications), this means that more than a single MO level is involved. The numbers in Figure 10 correspond to the numbered elements discussed earlier in this chapter and in Chapter 6. Arrows show flow and sequence. When there is a double-ended arrow, this signifies the possibility of an iteration and revision of work done earlier.

Much of the discussion of how SONG works in single-business organizations (Chapter 7) applies to MOs. Rather than repeating the relevant material here, I will simply make reference to it.

In the prior year's final quarter, the same four preparatory tasks described in Chapter 7 are completed at the Corporate level. These are: developing initial provisional definitions of each SBU's business and the MO's overall business (1); determining the boundaries and form of each SBU and OU (2); developing a base future scenario(s) (4); and designing and instituting a strategic database (10). All the discussion of these in Chapters 6 and 7 is relevant, except that in an MO, there are multiple businesses and SBUs. The provisional business definitions are reviewed and possibly modified by each SBU's PG as it formulates the SBU Strategy.

An additional Corporate-level preparatory task is the formulation of MO objectives, strategies and expectations of each SBU (12). This work is done by the CEO and her/his direct reports, and is informed by the base future scenarios (10) and the strategic database (10). Typically the CEO's vision and aspirations are major factors in determining Corporate's objectives and strategies. Corporate's expectations of the various SBUs are about the role MO wants each SBU to play in the portfolio. For example, some SBUs are expected to be the principal cash generators. Others are expected to provide revenue growth. Others are being looked to as the primary source of profit or surplus. A few SBUs are expected to take the lead in MO renewal. SBU managers need to know what role their SBU is expected to play in the MO's portfolio before they begin to formulate their SBU Strategy Proposal.

By the end of the prior year, the CEO develops and writes the CEO's Provisional Strategic Guideline Statement (3). This document contains the same material described in Chapters 6 and 7 with the addition of Corporate Objectives, Strategies and Expectations (12). Distribution of the CEO's Provisional Strategic Guidelines to the heads of SBUs and Corporate Functions immediately after the New Year launches the next planning cycle.

In early January, a Planning Group (PG) is formed in each SBU, and an Operational Planning Group (OPG) is formed in each Corporate Function. Corporate distributes templates specifying the common formats desired for an SBU Strategy Proposal (13) and a Corporate Function Operating Plan Proposal or CFOPP (14). A uniform format with a common language (templates include explicit definition of terms) greatly facilitates learning and understanding by MO executives and other SBU managers, both for Corporate Interrogation and for the Corporate Scrum.

During the next 10–12 weeks, each PG formulates its proposed strategy and each OPG formulates its proposed plan. The process is the same as that described for SBU Strategic Plans (5) and for Operating Plans (6) in Chapter 6, except that action planning is focused at a higher, less detailed level. Little attention is paid to measures and monitoring. The OPGs begin their work about 3 weeks later than the PGs, because they need to understand SBUs' intended strategies and their resource requirements as part of their own planning framework.

By early April, all SBU Strategy Proposals (13) are submitted to Corporate for review prior to Corporate Interrogation (15). A half-day meeting is scheduled and conducted by corporate executives with the leaders of each SBU. These interrogation sessions are conducted between mid April and mid-May. Within a week of each session, any desired modifications to an SBU Strategy Proposal is communicated by corporate executives to the SBU head. The SBU's PG is immediately reconvened to modify its proposed strategy in anticipation of the Corporate Scrum (17).

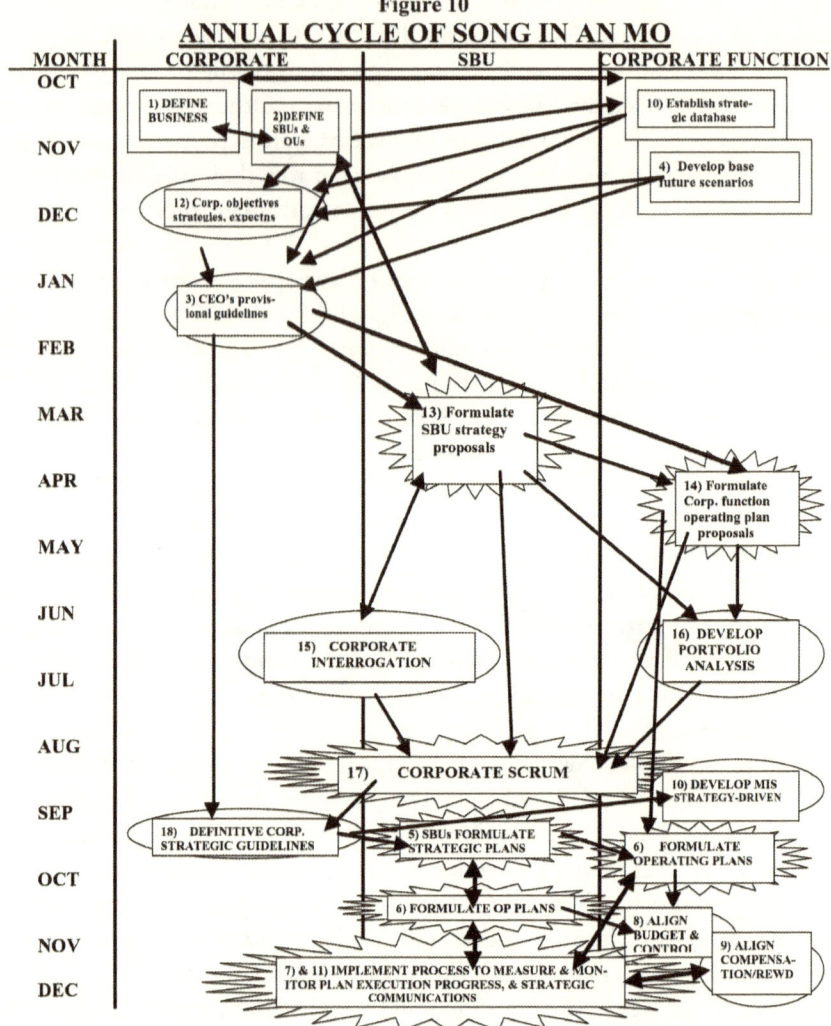

Figure 10
ANNUAL CYCLE OF SONG IN AN MO

While SBU Strategy Proposals are being recast, the Corporate Finance Function works together with the Corporate Planning Function to develop a Portfolio Analysis (14). Each SBU's projected performance and resource requirements is a key input to this work, as is also any required resources specified in CFOPPs. Concurrently, several Discussion Papers are developed as inputs to the Scrum, under supervision of Corporate Planning.

A 3-day Corporate Scrum (17) is conducted by the end of June for all senior corporate executives, all SBU heads plus two or three other key managers from each

SBU, and all Corporate Function chiefs. About two weeks prior to the Scrum, each participant receives a Scrum Workbook (prepared and distributed by Corporate Planning) containing all the inputs to the Scrum. Participants study this material prior to the Scrum and note questions, concerns and issues, so that formal presentations at the Scrum can be minimized and discussions will be productive.

Immediately after the Corporate Scrum, the CEO and other key corporate executives meet to decide which SBU Strategy Proposals and CFOPPs to approve as submitted, and which must be modified and in what way. Decisions are also made about how to allocate resources. Decisions are made about which MO issues identified at the Scrum will be addressed, how, when and with what accountability. Also, corporate objectives, strategies and expectations articulated in the CEO's Provisional Strategic guidelines (3) are reviewed and modified in light of the Scrum. All these decisions and their implications are then made explicit and documented in a CEO's Definitive Corporate Strategic Guideline Statement (18). This is distributed to all SBUs and Corporate Functions by mid-July.

Between mid-July and the end of August, each SBU's PG makes whatever modifications are necessary to align its Strategic Business Plan (5) with the Definitive Corporate Strategic Guidelines (18). Concurrently, each Corporate Function's OPG makes whatever modifications are necessary to align its Operating Plan (6) with the Definitive Corporate Strategic Guidelines. PGs and OPGs also develop more detailed action plans, measures and monitoring plans, and a communications plan. Definitive strategic and functional operating plans are published and distributed by the end of August.

Wherever a Strategic Business Plan (5) requires one or more supporting Operating Plans (6), these requirements are defined by the end of August and OPGs are formed. These groups complete their operating plans by the end of October, applying the process described in Chapter 6.

Implementation of both strategic and operating plans begins in early November, applying the Process for Measuring and Monitoring Implementation Progress and Updating Plans (7) and Strategy-Driven Communications (11) described in Chapter 6. Each SBU's PG monitors its Strategic Business Plan, and each OPG monitors its Operating Plan (both for SBUs' operating systems and for Corporate Functions). Corporate executives oversee this process, and monitor the progress of Corporate strategy and the achievement of Corporate strategic objectives.

Concurrently in November and December, Corporate Functions work to modify Budgeting Systems and Financial Controls (8), Compensation and Reward Systems (9), and MIS (10), to begin to bring them into closer alignment with current strategy. It is also during this period that next year's budget is prepared, using action plans and projected financial summaries in both strategic and operating plans as the basis for development.

During this fourth quarter, corporate executives again meet to review definitions of businesses and of SBUs and OUs and to reconsider corporate objectives, strategies and expectations. Concurrently, a specially selected management team reviews and perhaps reformulates the Base Future Scenario(s). And the CEO prepares another Provisional Strategic Guideline Statement to launch next year's planning cycle. All the while, current strategies and plans are being implemented and modified to ensure that they remain on target and on course.

NOTES TO CHAPTER 9

1 The Corporate Scrum is a process I invented together with colleagues. I have used the term scrum after the event in the game of rugby when a play arises out of a seemingly chaotic struggle.

CHAPTER 10

HOW SONG HELPS ENSURE TRUE SUCCESS

Any organization, not-for-profit, for profit or government, can achieve true success. This happens when its management consistently over time sets and achieves appropriate objectives … goals that are in tune both with the realities of its organization's capabilities and external environment, and with the aspirations and interests of its leaders and stakeholders. Management is able to do all this once it institutes a System for Organizational Navigation and Guidance (SONG) and learns how to use it skillfully as a core process for managing its business(es) and organization.

Salient Characteristics of SONG

SONG is a core management *system and process*. It is *applied continuously* in periodic cycles. It is *dynamic* in that its framework accommodates changes both within the organization and in its external environment. It is *systemic* in the way it treats the organization within its environmental context, and addresses the problems of changing the manner in which the organization works so as better to support plan execution. It is *outside->in driven* in that what goes on outside the organization sets the context and is the starting point of the SONG process. Such a perspective encourages objectivity in drawing conclusions from analyses and choosing strategic options. With this perspective, SONG's outlook is initially strategic, then tactical.

SONG is highly *participative*, encouraging broad personal involvement at every organizational level. Conclusions and decisions benefit from a multiplicity of informed inputs. A broad base of understanding and commitment is established within the organization for plan implementation. With its reliance on groups [Planning Groups (PGs), Operational Planning Groups (OPGs,) senior executives, etc.] SONG encourages formation of *coalitions* of managers and executives from different parts of the organization with different interests and agendas, working together to achieve common goals. With such focus, this diversity stimulates creative thinking in formulating and executing plans. In SONG, *everyone wears two hats*. This means that everyone involved views things from the perspective both of a business and of the organization as a whole. This characteristic is especially pronounced in multi-business organizations.

SONG is *iterative*. It enables conclusions and decisions to change and improve as new inputs and understandings are applied. Influence for decision-making flows *both top->down and bottom->up*. This means that although the initial framework for setting objectives and selecting strategies is established by the CEO in the Provisional Strategic Guidelines which are disseminated downwards, PGs in Strategic Business Units (SBUs) can "push back" and challenge elements of this framework as strategic plans are formulated. Further, as operating plans are developed to support an SBU's strategy, an OPG can "push back" and challenge certain conclusions and choices made by the SBU's PG.

Finally, SONG is *issue centered*, yet *integrative*. All the work done in SONG is focused on identifying, addressing and resolving issues in ways that take everyone's interests into account. What opportunities and potential problems are there in the organization's external environment? Which of these are worth pursuing and addressing? How, when and by whom? How can the organization's capabilities be leveraged? How can the organization's problems be offset or corrected? What changes are necessary to the way the organization works so that strategy implementation is successful? How can such changes be accomplished durably? How can organizational focus be sustained to ensure successful plan implementation? How can existing organizational systems be better aligned to support current strategies and plans? How can the different objectives, interests and agendas of Corporate and the SBUs be reconciled and aligned in the best interests of both parties?

SONG Leverages the Drivers for True Success

Used intelligently and creatively, SONG enables management to leverage four forces that drive true success. SONG provides the means to scan continuously an organization's external environment to identify and *understand* compelling facts and trends about its industry, markets, competitors, regulators, suppliers and funders, and thus identify probable future developments in scenarios. Management is also enabled to scan continuously its organization to identify and *understand* its capabilities and dysfunctions.

With these understandings and SONG, management then periodically and regularly *identifies attractive opportunities and alarming warning signals*, formulating *plans* to pursue selected opportunities and address the warning signals. Finally, SONG enables management to sustain *organizational focus* so crucial for executing its plans successfully.

By enabling management to focus on, influence and leverage the four key drivers for true success, SONG is management's most potentially powerful instrument for actually achieving true success. In order for this potential power to become real, management needs to learn how to use SONG skillfully.

SONG Promotes and Enhances Organizational Learning

SONG becomes increasingly powerful over time in helping to ensure true success. This is so because it provides an extremely effective framework and mechanism for organizational learning, applied repeatedly in cycles. Its systematic and comprehensive approach to measuring and monitoring progress and achievements as strategic and operating plans are executed, provides management with feedback on the *quality* of its plans and implementation efforts. This learning from implementation experience enables management to improve the quality of its plans and implementation efforts in the next cycle. Furthermore, SONG's participative approach to plan formulation and execution ensures that organizational learning is widespread and enduring.

Even in its initial application, SONG helps management formulate high quality plans and implement them effectively. Early focus on provisional definition of the business plus the CEO's Provisional Strategic Guidelines coupled with the Base Future Scenario(s) provide an SBU's PG with an outside->in context and comprehensive, objective external information for the Strategic Business Plan. A PG comprised of representatives from every important organizational function working together ensures an integrated approach to planning resulting in congruent strategies for products and services, markets, technology, operations, finance and the organization. These plus required rationales for strategic choices and detailed action plans provide a sound basis for successful plan execution. The likelihood of effective implementation is furthered by the formation of a coalition of key managers in the PG with the understanding, commitment and power to make the strategy happen.

When separate operating plans are needed to support the strategic plan, SONG helps ensure that these, too, are of high quality. Initial focus is on defining operating system(s) that need to be changed to work in new ways. This establishes a potent perspective for the operating plan. An internal scan of the operating system and how it works provides comprehensive, objective information for the OPG to identify high leverage targets on which to focus its change efforts. By identifying operating system priorities from an analysis of demands made on the operating system by the strategic business plan, alignment with that plan is ensured along with an outside->in, objective perspective. An OPG comprised of managers and supervisors from every key function within the operating system working together, ensures an integrative and realistic approach to planning. This plus required rationales for strategic choices and detailed action plans provide a sound basis for successful plan execution. The likelihood of effective implementation is furthered by the formation of a coalition of key managers and supervisors in the OPG with the understanding, commitment and power to make their plan happen.

SONG heightens the probability that both strategic and operating plans will be successfully implemented. Individuals are assigned accountability for clearly defined tasks and deliverables. Measures are applied to track progress and accomplishment. A systematic monitoring process is instituted involving all key managers with accountability meeting together at regular intervals. They share information about achievements, problems encountered and results from the application of measures. Then they identify learning from their implementation experience and apply this to updating and modifying their plans to ensure that they remain on target and on course.

Organizational learning stemming from all of the above also helps CEOs and other senior executives set more appropriate objectives. As experience with SONG accumulates over time, organizational leaders gain increased understanding of both external and internal realities. Better knowledge of industry, market and competitor trends along with relevant developments in the social-economic-political-technological environment enables better identification of opportunities and threats. Better knowledge of the organization's true capabilities and dysfunctions enables more realistic assessment of what can actually be achieved.

SONG's Contribution to True Success

In summary, SONG adds enormous value to any organization, enabling its management to achieve true success.

- It provides a strong, consistent outside->in perspective that enhances understanding of external realities and fosters objectivity

- It provides a systematic, integrated approach to planning that enables trade-offs among customer satisfaction, product and service design and delivery, quality, costs and productivity.
- It provides a dynamic approach to planning and implementation, anticipating and responding to changing market and customer needs and competitors' actions.
- It provides a way to get everyone in the organization to understand, buy-into, commit and do what is required.
- It provides a framework and mechanisms for continuous organizational learning.
- It fosters the setting of appropriate objectives.
- It enables multi-business organizations to reconcile and align objectives and strategies among SBUs and between SBUs and Corporate, to allocate resources effectively, and to leverage synergies.
- It enhances the probability that all plans will be executed successfully.

Because SONG has all these attributes, it provides executives and managers with a key to true success for both their organizations and themselves

Clearly, establishing SONG in an organization and working with it over time is a complex and demanding undertaking. It is not a quick fix. But the difficulties of changing the way organizations work are so great that to surmount these takes a multifaceted, systemic approach. A substantial investment in SONG will yield a substantial return in the form of durable improvement in organizational performance.

APPENDIX A

FOLLOWING UP A SAMPLE OF "EXCELLENT" COMPANIES

The Original Sample and Criteria for Selection

In their best selling book, *In Search of Excellence*, (Harper and Row, New York, 1982), T.J. Peters and R. H. Waterman, Jr. reported the results of research they and their colleagues conducted from 1977–81. They studied 62 large U.S. business corporations perceived as excellent and innovative by "an informed group of observers of the business scene ... business men, consultants, members of the business press and business academics". "Innovative" companies were defined as being "especially adroit at continually responding to change of any sort in their environments". The researchers excluded from consideration any companies in industries subject to governmental regulation.

As a criterion of business performance, Peters and Waterman specified that an "excellent" company had to be in the top half of its industry in four out of six measures of performance over a twenty-year period (1961–1980). These were: compounded asset growth; compounded equity growth; the ratio of market to book value; and returns on capital, equity and sales. All these are financial performance measures.

In addition, the researchers sought subjective ratings of innovativeness from "industry experts". Extensive interviews and business literature studies were conducted for each of the 62 companies deemed to be "excellent". The interviews focused on the "7-S Framework", a concept developed out of the initial phase of the research by McKinsey consultants (McKinsey is one of the world's leading management consulting firms). This framework suggests that it is useful to think about organizing as the inter-relations and interaction among seven factors ... organizational structure, strategy, systems, shared values, skills, management style, and staff.

Excellent Company Traits

From the research, Peters and Waterman concluded that each "excellent" company exhibited most of eight traits:

1. *A bias for action* ... getting on with it; not getting bogged down in analysis.

2. *Close to the customer* ... customer-centered orientation; lots of attention to and learning from customers.

3. *Autonomy and entrepreneurship* ... nurturing and supporting internal innovators and champions of new ideas and projects.

4. *Productivity through people* ... focus on and valuing people as a prime company asset, the root source of improvements in quality and productivity.

5. *Hands -on, value-driven* ... executives and managers at every level keep in close personal touch with day-to-day activities; company values and philosophy play a major part in day-to-day choices and decisions.

6. *Stick to the knitting* ... avoid straying too far afield from the business(es) which are well known to and form the basis of the firm.

7. *Simple form, lean staff* ... organization structure is simple, not complex, with a minimal group of executives and staff at the top.

8. *Simultaneous loose-tight properties* ... organization is both centralized and decentralized, with much decision-making pushed down to lower levels, but with critical issues decided at the top.

Following Up to Test the Validity of This Success Definition

If all of the above criteria were truly valid indicators of organizational success, then the companies in Peters' and Waterman's sample should look and be as successful decades later as they were in 1981. This should be especially true of 14 firms in a group that were identified as "exemplars" because they "represent especially well both sound performance and the eight traits we have identified".

In early 1996 using performance data published in *Fortune* magazine, I followed up 48 of Peters and Waterman's 62 "excellent" companies. Data on the other 14 firms were unavailable, either because of mergers that had occurred since 1981, or because a few of these firms are privately held and hence public information is scarce.

Follow Up Criteria

In my follow-up, I applied six of the *Fortune* criteria which echo those applied by Peters and Waterman:

1. *Total return to investors* ... includes both share price appreciation and dividend yield: <u>company's return must be at least 120% of the Fortune 500 median for the annual average rate for the years 1986–96</u> (The Fortune 500 is a ranking by total revenues of the U.S.' 500 largest industrial firms).

2. *Earning per share growth* ... growth in primary earnings per share as shown on the income statement, adjusted for stock splits and stock dividends: <u>company is in the top 50 of the Fortune 500 for the years 1986–96.</u>

3. *Market value added* ... MVA is a measure of how much wealth a company creates or destroys; it is computed by combining a company's debt with the market value of its stock, and then subtracting the capital that has been invested in the company: <u>company is ranked in the top 200 of 1000 of the U.S.' largest industrial firms (in terms of total revenues).</u>

4. *Increase in MVA* ... <u>company's MVA ranking has improved consistently since 1985.</u>

5. *Customer satisfaction* ... an index (1–100 derived from an econometric model of U.S. consumers' responses to 17 questions in telephone surveys of about 30000 actual users of 3900 products and services, conducted by the University of Michigan Business School and the American Society for Quality Control; questions are about perceptions of service, quality, value and how well the product or service lived up to expectations, how it compared to an ideal, and how willing people were to pay more for it: <u>company must score higher than 107% of the national average.</u>

6. *Company reputation* … an index derived from an annual survey of the perceptions of more than 10000 U.S. senior executives, outside directors and financial analysts of 395 large U.S. companies: perceptions are about quality of management, quality of products and services; innovativeness; long-term investment value; financial soundness; ability to attract, develop and keep talented people; responsibility to the community and the environment; and wise use of corporate assets: company is ranked in the top 125 of the "most admired".

In Table 1 we see how the 48 "excellent" companies met the above six criteria positively, and how the "exemplar" companies fared as well.

TABLE 1

Positive Performance of "Excellent" Companies (15 years later)

NUMBER CRITERIA MET	48 EXCELLENT COS		14 "EXEMPLAR" COS	
6	0	0.0%	0	0.0%
5	6	12.5%	3	21.4%
4	4	8.3%	3	21.4%
3	9	18.8%	2	14.3%
2	7	14.6%	2	14.3%
1	7	14.6%	1	7.1%
0	6	12.5%	2	14.3%
Insufficient Data	9	18.8%	1	7.1%

In Table 2 we see how many of these same companies performed very negatively against these same criteria.

TABLE 2

Negative Performance of "Excellent" Companies (15 years later)

NUMBER OF CRITERIA STRONGLY NEGATIVE	48 EXCELLENT COMPANIES		14 "EXEMPLAR COS.	
6	0	0.0%	0	0.0%
5	3	6.3%	2	14.3%
4	1	2.1%	0	0.0%
3	5	10.4%	1	7.1%
2	3	6.3%	0	0.0%
1	13	27.1%	4	28.6%
0	15	31.3%	6	42.9%
Insufficient data	8	16.7%	1	7.1%

From Table 1, we see that less than 40% of the 48 "excellent" companies met three or more of the six criteria. Only one in five met four or more criteria. More than one out of four, however, met only one or none of the criteria. From Table 2 we see that 25% of these same companies had two or more serious performance problems.

The "exemplar" companies fared somewhat better. More than half met three or more of the criteria. Yet more than one in five had two or more serious performance problems.

TABLE 3
Correlation of Most Admired Companies With Other Criteria

NUMBER EXCELLENT COMPANIES

Meet Most Admired & 2/4 or More Objective Performance Criteria	Meet Both Most Admired & Cust. Satisf. Criteria
19/48 or 40%	9/15* or 60%

* Data available for only 15/48 excellent companies

In mid 2005, I again followed up the performance of the 62 companies. By this time, some 25 years after the selection of "excellent" companies, I was able to make the following observations:

- 21 companies (36%) no longer existed; 12 had been acquired and 9 had failed

- 5 companies were privately held; no performance data was available

- of the 36 remaining companies, no more than 33% could be considered superior performers, applying the criteria described above

- of the 13 publicly held "exemplar" companies, one had been acquired; only 3 (23%) could be considered superior performers

APPENDIX B

GENERIC STRATEGIC OPTIONS FOR SBUs

1. DEVELOP INITIAL MARKET FOR A NEW OFFERING

Create initial demand and a new market for a genuinely new offering for which no precedent exists (e.g. "instant" photography in 1949).

2. PENETRATE EXISTING MARKET(S)

Grow revenues and market share with existing offerings in existing markets by focusing on advertising, promotion, pricing, alliances, channels and/or acquisitions.

3. REPOSITION IN MARKET(S)

Change market share (up or down) by offering or withdrawing new, enhanced or existing products and services using more or less existing or new channels, to more or less existing or new markets.

4. INCREASE CAPACITY BEYOND PRESENT NEEDS

Add capacity ... production, distribution, sales, service, management ... beyond current needs to improve competitive position and enhance readiness to capitalize on new opportunities.

5. GRANT/ACQUIRE LICENSES

domestic or foreign ... to market own or other organizations' products and services.

6. INFLUENCE SUPPLIERS' BEHAVIOR

by negotiation, education & training, investment or acquisition ... to enhance market offerings,reduce costs or form alliances for mutual benefit.

7. INFLUENCE CUSTOMER OR CHANNEL BEHAVIOR

by solving their problems and by special inducements ... to achieve mutually beneficial objectives.

8. CHANGE STANCE TOWARD REGULATORS OR FUNDERS

by enhancing relationships, lobbying, litigation, applying influence ... to reduce constraints, to achieve more favorable climate and to gain support.

9. RESTRUCTURE ORGANIZATION

Change organizational design (SBU, functional, matrix), redefine SBU scope, add/reduce levels,eliminate, add, redefine functions ... to improve effectiveness in strategy formulation & execution.

10. ENHANCE EXISTING MARKET OFFERINGS

Improve existing products and services with new features, better prices, higher quality and/or better distribution.

11. CUT BACK TO THE MOST DESIRABLE CORE

Eliminate all but the most desirable lines of business ... sell market share by increasing prices and reduce spending on marketing, sales and service.

12. DEFER INVESTMENT

Run a tight ship and postpone any investments for the future.

13. DEVELOP A BUSINESS ABROAD

in markets with characteristics different from domestic ones ... using existing or modified products and services.

14. ESTABLISH OFF-SHORE FACILITIES FOR THE EXISTING SBU

for production, sales, distribution, marketing, customer service ... to reduce operating costs or for political and/or foreign exchange or tax reasons.

15. EXPAND GEOGRAPHICALLY WITHIN DOMESTIC MARKET

by branching, franchising, acquisitions, etc.

16. RATIONALIZE INTERNAL OPERATIONS

Improve capacity utilization, layouts, workflows and simplify work processes and apply standardization, mechanization and automation.

17. INVEST IN INFORMATION AND OTHER TECHNOLOGY

for more effective and efficient use of facilities, work processes, equipment, management information, distribution, marketing and sales.

18. IMPROVE OVERALL OPERATING EFFECTIVENESS

through better use of strategic management, improved functional/departmental integration, process redesign and capitalizing on opportunities for economies of scale and synergy.

19. OUTSOURCE OPERATIONS

identify and contract with other organizations, domestic or foreign, operational segments in order to lower total costs, improve delivery reliability & flexibility, and/or to improve quality

APPENDIX C

GENERIC STRATEGIC OPTIONS FOR OPERATING PLANS

1. SIMPLIFY THE PRODUCT LINE/RANGE OF SERVICES

To achieve efficiencies in marketing, selling, operations, inventories, distribution and servicing, reduce the number and diversity of market offerings.

2. UPGRADE EXISTING PHYSICAL FACILITIES

To improve quality of market offerings, the work environment and to reduce operating costs, improve the existing physical facilities.

3. IMPROVE EQUIPMENT AND PROCESS TECHNOLOGY

Invest in better equipment and processes to improve quality of market offerings, increase capacity, increase flexibility for changes in market offerings and capacity, and reduce costs.

4. INCREASE MECHANIZATION

Substitute machines for people wherever possible to achieve more consistent quality and reduce payroll cost.

5. INCREASE CAPACITY

Expand physical facilities, increase throughput or expand the ability of service,to improve responsiveness to anticipated market demand, provide more comprehensive services, reduce overtime, improve layouts and achieve economies of scale.

6. OPTIMIZE MAKE/BUY MIX

Change the balance between what is purchased from outside the organization and what is produced internally in order to increase the value-added, improve quality, reduce total costs,use available capacity and/or improve reliability of delivering offerings to the marketplace.

7. IMPROVE VENDORS' QUALITY

Work with vendors and suppliers of materials, components, and services to improve their quality and reliability in order to improve the quality of market offerings, reduce total costs and improve reliability of delivery.

8. IMPROVE DISTRIBUTION

Reshape distribution network, policies and practices to in crease responsiveness to markets, focus on highest profit outlets, and reduce inventory, transportation and storage costs.

9. IMPROVE ENERGY UTILIZATION EFFICIENCY

Upgrade or replace existing facilities and equipment to achieve greater energy efficiency, reduce energy losses by insulation, recycling, etc., improve energy controls and convert to lower cost energy sources.

10. REDUCE MATERIAL LOSSES

Invest in systems, procedures and methods to reduce waste, material obsolescence and to lower cost of purchased material.

11. IMPROVE WORK METHODS AND PROCEDURES

Streamline and increase the efficiency of how work gets done by applying concepts and techniques from industrial and manufacturing engineering and operations research.

12. IMPROVE EQUIPMENT UTILIZATION

Increase throughput and return on investment by improving planning and scheduling, using excess capacity, ensuring conformance to operating standards and preventive maintenance.

13. INCREASE STANDARDIZATION IN OPERATIONS

Invest in standardizing the way work gets done in order to simplify processes, procedures and practices, reduce inventories and costs, improve quality and reliability of offerings and improving responsiveness to customers.

14. IMPROVE INFORMATION HANDLING

Streamline methods and procedures for handling information and processing data to reduce clerical costs and errors and to improve response time between data inputs and outputs.

15. IMPROVE DESIGN OF MARKET OFFERINGS

Develop new or modified designs for products and services that will improve responsiveness to customer requirements, improve quality and reliability, and lower total costs.

16. IMPROVE MANAGEMENT INFORMATION

Improve the relevance, comprehensiveness, accuracy and timeliness of information that management needs for better decisions and control.

17. IMPROVE LEVERAGE FROM REWARDS AND PENALTIES

Improve employee motivation by systematically and consistently providing and withholding appropriate rewards and compensation and by applying discipline and termination.

18. IMPROVE COMMUNICATIONS

Improve employees' (and appropriate outsiders') understanding of what they are doing and how this supports the organization's objectives, strategies and plans by providing better information, by opening up new vertical and lateral channels, by listening more attentively and by making better use of various media.

19. DEVELOP A MULTIPLE, FLEXIBLY SKILLED WORKFORCE

Improve selection procedures and upgrade peoples' skills to optimize ability to match work with people, and improve organizational flexibility and responsiveness to market needs.

20. IMPROVE MANAGEMENT COMPETENCE AND CAPABILITIES

Improve selection procedures and provide training and development activities to managers and supervisors.

21. REDUCE LOST WORK TIME

Improve policies, procedures, systems and they way these are implemented to minimize time spent away from work because of illness, accidents, grievances and personal reasons.

22. REDESIGN JOBS

Make jobs more challenging and satisfying by enlarging range of tasks and responsibilities and by incorporating functions being handled by other groups, to reduce total costs, improve quality, enhance motivation and improve organizational responsiveness.

23. IMPROVE PERFORMANCE OF INDIVIDUAL DEPARTMENTS

Improve quality of staff, organization and/or methods, procedures and processes within a department to upgrade its effectiveness and that of the organization as a whole.

24. CHANGE ORGANIZATIONAL STRUCTURE

Change relative status of functions, regroup functional responsibilities, eliminate levels, clarify chains-of-command and change spans of control in order to enhance market responsiveness, improve total organizational effectiveness, reduce total costs and provide more strategic focus.

25. IMPROVE INTEGRATION AMONG FUNCTIONS

Break down walls between departments/functions to improve coordination and cooperation, provide ways to reconcile conflicting interests, goals and priorities, and improve the effectiveness of business processes and the entire organization.

26.*IMPROVE UNION-MANAGEMENT RELATIONS; CHIP AWAY AT WORKFORCE-RELATED PRODUC- TIVITY PROBLEMS

Work with union leaders and use collective bargaining to achieve productivity gains and try to eliminate or modify restrictive work practices.

27. SHORTEN TIME-TO-MARKET FOR NEW OFFER- INGS

Redesign business processes, systems and procedures and functional inter-relationships to shorten time required from the initial concept to delivery to the first customer of new market offerings, to improve responsiveness to market needs and opportunities.

28. SHORTEN ORDER-TO-DELIVERY TIME FOR CUR- RENT OFFERINGS

Redesign business processes, systems and procedures and functional inter-relationships to shorten time required from the placement of a customer's order to its delivery, to improve responsiveness to customers and reduce inventory costs.

29. SHORTEN PROVISIONING TIME

Redesign internal business processes and work with a reduced number of suppliers of materials, components and services to minimize time between provisioning and actual need, to minimize inventories and throughput time.

30.*ENGAGE IN PRODUCTIVITY BARGAINING

Plan and negotiate a comprehensive, "win-win" bargaining package to elimi-nate/modify formal contract provisions and/or informal "custom and practice" understandings to open up new opportunities for productivity improvement based on specific activity changes by the workforce.

31. ESTABLISH A PROGRAM FOR TOTAL QUALITY CONTROL AND IMPROVEMENT

Develop, train for and apply systems, procedures and methods for establishing that everyone is responsible for quality and for achieving maximum employee involvement in pursuing quality perfection.

32. ENCOURAGE EMPLOYEE INVOLVEMENT

Establish and train joint voluntary employee/management groups to identify and recommend changes both in the way work is done and in the work environment aimed at improving both the quality of time spent working and the quality of market offerings, thus enhancing productivity and employee satisfaction.

33.*INSTITUTE EMPLOYEE INVOLVEMENT WITH GAINS SHARING FOR PRODUCTIVITY IMPROVE-MENT

Establish a formal program (e.g. Scanlon, Rucker, Improshare, etc.) to generate labor cost (and related) savings through voluntary participative problem-solving groups involving both employees and management, and then share frequently any resulting cash benefits according to an agreed formula .

* These options are applicable only in situations where there are trade unions involved.

ABOUT THE AUTHOR

Since 1958, Mr. Judson has been advising managements of businesses, not-for-profit organizations, and government ministries and agencies in North and Latin America, Europe and the Middle-East, helping them to develop and implement strategies to improve business and organizational performance. From 1962 to 1966, he was a management consultant with The Emerson Consultants in London, England. From 1966 to 1976 he was on the senior staff of Arthur D. Little, Inc. He was one of the founders of The Berwick Group in 1976, of Gray-Judson in 1981, and of The Judson Company in 1994.

Mr. Judson helped achieve lasting changes in manufacturing and service organizations in many industries ... aerospace, computers and electronics, oil and gas, forest products, chemicals and photography, pharmaceuticals, consumer packaged goods, telecommunications, financial services, mining, transportation, utilities and advertising ... by developing innovations in products and services, business processes and operating methods. In the non-profit sector, he worked with trade unions, social agencies, museums and performing arts organizations. His work focused on the design, development and implementation of strategic planning and management processes and the improvement of both productivity and quality of working life. He has been especially concerned with helping managements and their organizations to develop a continuing ability to learn from their experiences, and then apply that learning to improve both business and operating performance and the quality of working life for employees at every level.

His Bachelor's and Master's degrees are from the Massachusetts Institute of Technology ... one in Chemical Engineering and the other in Organizational Behavior and Industrial Relations. After two years with U.S.Rubber Company as a production foreman, he joined Polaroid Corporation where he set up and managed the Personnel Department. He then worked with the transition of new products, from R&D into manufacturing, and managed a new photographic film manufacturing plant. In his last four years at Polaroid, Mr. Judson was the first Corporate Director of Training and Development.

Mr. Judson also taught management courses at Northeastern University and has led seminars and workshops in strategic planning and strategic management, productivity improvement, change management and in interviewing techniques throughout the United States and Canada, and in the United Kingdom, Europe and Iran. He was a senior faculty member at the Arthur D. Little Management Education Institute, in a graduate Master's degree program for advanced managers from developing nations. He is the author of *A Manager's Guide to Making Changes* (John Wiley & Sons, London, 1966), and has also had papers published in the *Harvard Business Review, The Technology Review, The Journal of Business Strategy* and in several other professional journals. His books, *Making Strategy Happen: Transforming Plans Into Reality* and *Changing Behavior in Organizations* were published by Blackwell Publishers (Oxford, U.K.) in 1996 and 1991 respectively.

From 1984–2001, Mr. Judson was a member of the Board of Directors and Chairman since 1992 of Greater Boston Rehabilitation Services, Inc., a non-profit human service agency providing vocational rehabilitation to people with emotional and other disabilities. Since 1996, he has worked with the Executive Service Corps, consulting with non-profit organizations. He is a member of The University Club of Boston. For most of his life, he has been deeply involved with music, both as a pianist and as a composer.

978-0-595-40526-8
0-595-40526-6